MAKE UP NOT REQUIRED

How to Brand the TRUE YOU

LaurieAnn Campbell
Co-authored with Robert Max Wall

10-10-10
Publishing

Publisher
10-10-10 Publishing
Markham, ON Canada

Printed in Canada and the United States of America

Table of Contents

ACKNOWLEDGMENTS

To my parents, Lachlan Ross Campbell and Pauline Serret-Campbell – I can't even start to tell you how many times I have been grateful for you just supporting me in my crazy ventures! In all my ventures. I love you so much! And Mommy and Daddy, as I still like to call you, I have learned so much from you. To Dad… yes, I am the turtle. And yes, I will get to that finish line before the hare. Thank you for that story; and I don't mind being called a "turtle."

Robert Wall – A huge thanks for your contribution to this book as my co-author. I have waited 15 years to make this happen. Thank you for helping me do that by sharing your insight!!

Raymond Aaron – Thank you so much for teaching me so much about my book not just being a "book" but something so much more. Raymond, you have been tough on me, but for a reason. But your delivery is also kind and understanding. I learned so much from you!

To my sisters, Janet Campbell and Donella Campbell – For loving me no matter what. You know how much you have been there for me. I hope I have been there as much for you too. I love you with all my heart.

To my daughter, Nikki Morrison – For being there for me through the toughest times. I thank you for your determination and your belief in me, even when you saw me at my lowest. Nikki, thank you also for the book cover picture. You inspire me every day. From your Plastic Waste Awareness to your photography and your videography. Even more, your determination, evident now that you have become an Electrical Engineer after completing your Psychology B.A. at Carleton. I love you Nikki, for believing in me and being there for me. I leaned on you at an age I shouldn't have, but you were, and still are, my rock. My love for you is forever.

To my son Brendon – I love you. I know motherhood has been something you wonder about. There are no "absolutes." Where you feel I failed, you are right. I don't have a roadmap to motherhood. But Brendon, thank you for your "love you tons mom" messages over the years of me finding myself. They meant the WORLD to me.

To my son Lachlan – Thank you for your patience, and for visiting me when I ran away from pain. It wasn't you I was running away from. It was the emptiness of not having you there every day. You still came to hang out in the summers with me at my new place and that is so appreciated. A mother is never perfect. I will tell you though, my unconditional love for you is. And I will never forget the support and love you gave me.

Brent Pearce - For the years you were there and believed in me. I am so appreciative of your university students helping me out through YOUR guidance. I was 18 when I met you and you always believed in me. Thank you. I am so honoured that you are Hampy's Godfather. I am also honoured to still be in touch with you!

Wayne Clancy - My friend, my support, and my inspiration as I have watched you grow from when we first met to become a very successful entrepreneur and author. You taught me that DREAMS can become REALITY.

Bart Baggett – One of the toughest coaches you will have side by side with Raymond. Bart, you will not let me be less than I am. Sometimes that stings, but it has a purpose. Thank you for also believing in me, regardless of my "wimpy" nature sometimes. You have to go with the "punches" if you will make it. You taught me that.

Doc Grayson – My kind mentor. The person there for me when I needed to call out for help. You believed in me all the way along my path. I love you Doc. You are such a positive and inspiration person!

Roy Miller – Thank you for listening to me no matter what. I am so excited to see your book come to fruition. Chocolate Chip Cookies – Comfort Foods and Death Bed Wishes. You are truly inspiring and a great friend, and my partner in the Podcast, That Gal with That Guy. I so enjoy these.

Sumit – My new and wonderful partner in India. I love you son. I know you will be successful with your integrity, ambition and kindness. You are a great addition to my life. Thank you for being a part of our Podcast Sharing Your Thoughts! Love that we are an Indo-Canada community.

To Wendy Musch, Jennifer Kalz – My colleagues and friends who are a part of this book, thank you for your inspiration and support to see me to the end of it, and your contribution! I really enjoy our evenings on www.advancedbrandingcollaborative.com.

Charles DeVries – My sideline friend who is always there when I need him, and as well, part of my team in graduating from the Master's Certified Handwriting Analysis course. Without you, Charles, I don't know if I would have completed it. We complimented each other in that aspect – collaboration, and support.

Jim McNeil – A HUGE thank you! It was fate that I met you at a "free" live presentation about understanding about how to be a speaker. What I didn't know was that it I would go on to be a published author. Jim thank you for introducing me to Raymond Aaron. You are a wonderful person with an amazing story of your background, going from janitor to worldwide public speaker.

Jack Canfield – Thank you for your inspiration, your story, and your books, and sharing the idea that Quantum Physics is real. I loved *The Secret* and thank you for your input. I really enjoyed meeting you.

Forbes Riley – Your inspiration and belief in others to be able to conquer their fears and reach out and build themselves as "winners" is amazing. I thank you for that.

To my pets – Rolly and Bingbing (my dogs) and Loki, Calie, Batcat, Snowball, Chesha (my cats), and Hashi (my fish). You are there in the morning, in the afternoon and at night, just excited to have me with you. Talk about unconditional love? And they are my brand. My love for animals.

To my ex's - I know this is a strange acknowledgment, but I can't do this without saying thank you to my ex-husband for assisting in my growth so that I could learn more about myself, and my abilities. He was tough, and I tried to be his best friend, but he didn't get that. But

I won't discount the fact that I learned from him and that he is a great father. To my ex-boyfriend, you taught me that we can be best friends, and in a relationship, and love each other, but that a long-distance relationship doesn't work in the end. I learned from my two most loved men in my life. In a different way. To my ex -husband, thank you for my children and lessons learned. To my Mau? Thank you for still being there when I need you.

Names I need to mention here too ...

Sylvia Morneau and Denise Powell – You have always been my longest best friends.

Laura Wilson – Thank you for being my new best friend. Proud of you lady!

Deanna Warne – Do you know why I have you here in my book? My partner, my friend, my family when I was away from mine.

Tony Junor and Rena Anderson – My Enterprise Centre dearest friends and still there for me.

Christine Blue – Love you friend.

Shari-Anne Way and Lisa Owens – Dear new friends and supportive!

Gloria Beale – For loving all my posts – you are a dear.

Hampy – My character I created. Always there for me. www.hampy.ca

And you can find me too at www.handwritingspeaksvolumes.com

Grace and perseverance…. This is what my friends, family and coaches have taught me.

From Robert Wall

To my wife, Kelli Ann Wall – Aside from my faith in God, you are my rock in this ever-changing world. 2012 was one of my hardest years, mentally, emotionally, and spiritually. You came into my life at the perfect time, and there has never been a setting of the sun when I haven't been grateful for our life or the love we share together and towards our miracle baby, Staci Ann (our Sesame). You are more than I could ever ask for in a wife; you serve and care for others alongside me, are one of the hardest working women I know. Your love as a mother cannot be matched. We are truly blessed. I love you.

To my children, Devin Michael and Chelsea Madigan – Although my work, business and studies stole many of those early years of time together, I always made sure you had everything you needed, including the comfort of knowing how much you were loved. Devin, you inspired me at such a young age to work hard for my family and to achieve every goal I set, not only for myself but also for those to whom I dedicated my life. I am immensely proud of the man you have become and look forward to celebrating all your future endeavours. Chelsea, my first daughter, my rose amongst the thorns. Chelsea, you brought a whole new meaning into my life. Born premature at just 3lbs and in the ICU for almost 2 months, God steadied my heart and began a transformation in my life for the better. You have had your challenges in life, but just like your first days spent in intensive care, you have overcome every obstacle placed in your path. Continue to believe in yourself, because so many others do. You are beautiful, respected by your family, and amongst your peers and loved deeply.

To my daughter in Heaven, Elizabeth Ann Wall, born July 5, 2001 and laid to rest on October 22, 2003 – As I push back the tears and begin to write, where do I even begin? Although those words still haunt me in my thoughts and dreams: "Mr. Wall, we do not know how to say this, but from everything we've observed, although we are still determining the type of birth defect, it is evident that your daughter is terminal and may not live past this week." Almost 2 ½ years later, you sure did prove them wrong. Lizzy, my angel, you not only changed my heart, in the way I treat others, and in my faith towards God, you impacted the lives of so many others around the world. You could not walk, talk, see, or even eat on your own, yet you are the true model of what a witness and servant is to God. Through your spiritual presence, your glowing smile, the strength you displayed through all you endured, and the abundant energy you produced in those around you... YOU, Elizabeth Ann Wall, delivered a message from Heaven and have actually made atheists see God. I love you and will continue to keep your work on earth alive through my testimonies, writings, and your life's story. Until we meet again.

To LaurieAnn Campbell - I would not be writing these acknowledgments without your invitation to contribute my insight to this book. Thank you so much for this opportunity, your inspiration and motivation to continue forward even in the foggiest of days. I pray this book brings joy and transformation into the hearts and minds of many. I am already looking forward to our next series together.

FOREWORD

Make Up Not Required – Branding The True YOU by LaurieAnn Campbell and co-authored by Robert Wall is intended to help you understand that you can achieve more success and happiness in your life if you explore your character to be able to brand the true YOU. This book is unique because it includes handwriting analysis and taking a pen to paper to learn more about yourself to build better self-confidence and success. The book also teaches you the values of how to build relationships, how to understand yourself better in dealing with relationships with yourself and your clients. This book will encourage you to allow yourself to challenge your beliefs, find your values, guide your life accordingly and learn to be yourself. By being truthful to yourself and others, you will find *huge* power and success. In this book:

You will explore the interlinking cycle of beliefs, values, actions and outcomes that reinforce each other

You will see that as you hone your skill at being authentic, you will start to become more powerful and that power feeds and supports your beliefs.

Raymond Aaron
New York Times Bestselling Author

"Be yourself;
everyone else is already taken."
— **Oscar Wilde**

CHAPTER 1

It's TRUE That Your Best Brand Is YOU
by LAURIEANN

This Is the Real Thing

YOU. It all starts there. Some of you may be wondering how it is that YOU can be the one that is special enough to be on the front end of your product. It's simple. It is a known fact that 80% of people will buy if they like you. So the goal here is to gain the trust of the people you want as your customers/clients, and the way to do this is to brand YOU.

What is so special about YOU? This is what this book will help you explore, determine, and define. Once you have completed all the chapters, you will not only understand, but you will also realize the validity in creating a brand around YOU; your name, your face, your character—YOU.

At first, this all seems a bit crazy, particularly if you are an introvert. It may seem impossible even. It is not impossible. All you need is some guidance. And once you put your mind to it and take action, it is incredible what results you will have.

When I started on this journey, I was coming out of a "rut." I had succeeded many times in my past, but at the time I found this method, I had been a recluse for almost 10 years for the most part. I had lost my business and nearly all my material possessions.

This led me to a lot of internal soul searching, not only on a personal basis but on a business basis as well. Who am I? Am I the person I was in my 30s and 40s, who was a go-getter and a doer, lit up with the desire to succeed? Or was I that failure who invested everything on a dream and lost it.

I felt as though I had let everyone down.

But it came down to this, the question: Why was I feeling like I let "everyone" down, but failed to look internally and ask myself who the person was that I was letting down the most?

In that moment, a very important answer came to me, and I realized that the most important person I was letting down was ME. You could say that that voice, that little "Jiminy Cricket," was saying exactly that. "LaurieAnn, it's not the others that matter. The person you are letting down is YOU."

And there is the YOU. That voice inside of you speaks to you quite often. It isn't like you are speaking to yourself and saying, "Who did I let down?" Often, when that voice is asking that question, it is in the second person. I believe this voice puts into perspective your ID speaking to you and telling you what you need to hear.

YOU!

With this, I began to seek more knowledge, more growth, and meditated on where I wanted to go and what I wanted to do. I had found a good-paying job, but I knew that was not my retirement plan. In fact, remaining in that job until I was 65 would not give me the retirement lifestyle that I wanted.

I was searching the WEB one day, when a face flashed across my screen. I was intrigued, so I clicked on it and watched the video. It was someone speaking on a topic, on exactly what I needed—branding. I had never heard of this person before, but it was serendipity.

Later, I joined a group that had just started, and began to delve into the areas I really needed to know more about. The group was called the AMC (Advanced Mastermind Collaborative). With this wonderful team, came the ABC (Advanced Branding Collaborative). As time went on, all the information led to where I needed to be.

I had two businesses I had been building quietly and slowly in the background, but I didn't have the key to promoting them. This is where clarity came in. I was focusing on the wrong thing. Instead of branding my businesses, I needed to start branding myself.

I became a founding partner, and it has become a wonderful journey.

In just a few months, I have not only found great friends and business partners, but I have also implemented all the learning into my other two businesses, and combined them into a beautiful little package that is now selling like I could not have imagined before.

I have also been asked to join my other mentor in assisting in leading groups for his coaching program, which I completed and is part of that "other business."

Why did my friends reach out and ask me to assist, when there are so many other potential candidates? Because I believe they saw me on my videos, noticed my ads, and were inspired by the fact that I was creating a brand for myself. Had I remained hidden and reclusive, this opportunity would never have arisen, nor would the sales in my own businesses.

It's time to come out and join the world for success. It's time to brand YOU. Be seen, share your passion, share your story, be genuine, be present. By following the plan below, you will find that once you implement these—and I highly recommend you do so while reading this book—by the end of this book, you will have seen so much progress that you will be in action mode. You will not want to stop.

It is TRUE that the best brand is YOU. Gain trust, gain fans, gain self-confidence, gain sales—but know that this is hard work. This is not something that will happen overnight. But with diligence, persistence, and an honest belief in yourself and this book, YOU will be the successful brand in front of your product.

YOU Are the One People Want to Get to Know

Don't underestimate the power of YOU. Your character is one of the most valuable assets you own. Why? Because once you are out there and people know you, you don't have to attach yourself to one product. You represent you, the person people know and trust, and whose opinion they value.

In order to do that, however, you must be willing to take time and build your presence online and in person. This is not something that will happen overnight. It won't even likely happen in a month, six months, or a year. But if you keep plugging away, or grinding as they say today, you will find that once you start moving into the second year, you will begin to see results.

Let's say you own a restaurant. People come to eat, and they like the atmosphere. But what would be even better to keep them coming back than just the food and atmosphere? YOU. When someone browses the internet for the best spot to eat, wouldn't you think they would be intrigued if the owner has on his blog or social media pages, his staff and him talking about them, and showing off their friendliness and their skills at cooking? Or even having a few regulars on the video to give testimonials, not just of the food and ambiance, but of the service and personal touch given to all aspects of the business?

When they can engage with your personality and they like you, as stated before, they will be more likely to buy, and also more likely to come back for more. YOU are a part of their experience.

This holds true for coaches, health professionals, real estate agents... you name it. It also holds true for people selling products! If YOU believe in what you are selling, you don't need to actually sell it. All you have to do is be out there telling everyone how wonderful this product is. This is often even more powerful when you can tell your audience that you own it, use it, eat it, wear it—whatever the product is.

The value of believing in yourself is augmented when you also believe in what you are presenting to your target market. And because YOU believe in it, so will they.

This is where your passion comes into play. Find what you are passionate about. Follow this by taking action.

But remember, this is not something that will happen overnight. Persistence and patience are two very important values to have. There will be days when you feel like you are going nowhere. But when those days arise, look back to a week, a month, or six months before you started on this journey, and you WILL see that your efforts will not have been in vain. Keep going and don't give up, because the best is yet to come.

So how do you get people to trust you and like you and become your fan?

Your Product Is Secondary to YOU

Put yourself before your product. This is very important if you are going to succeed at making money from multiple income streams. If your product is in front of you, when you add or move to another product, you will have to start all over again.

When you are in front of your product, when you introduce something new, your fans will follow you. You don't have to start all over again, you just add this to your list of "endorsements."

Further on in this book, there will be more information about how to stack your building blocks. And you are standing on top of each block you lay down. Be cautious, however, in how you do this. You need to do this, as the saying goes, one step at a time, one building block at a time. If you try to build it too quickly, it will likely crumble. You won't have the sound foundation needed to attain the height you want. This is again where patience is so important.

I remember when I purchased an existing business. People asked me if I was going to change the name. It was an auto repair company that had been in business for 10 years. I opted not to change the name, feeling that it had branded itself in those 10 years. In hindsight, I believe it would have been beneficial to change the name and to brand myself as the honest owner—a female owner, and someone to be trusted. Yes, hindsight is 20/20. Would it have made a difference? I don't know, but knowing what I know now, it may well have been the right thing to do.

For as long as I owned that business, I felt as though I was hiding under the name of someone I didn't even know. And in the end, the name meant nothing to the customers once the original owner had sold it to me. I would have had nothing to lose by changing it, and maybe even a lot to gain.

All this social media appearance and all the great platforms were available then too, but they were in the infancy stage then, and I didn't have the insight on how to maximize the potential. Now that I do, it's another story.

Would it have made a difference? I will never know. But it's an interesting thought.

The other thing I did that would have served me better to think first than do, was build too quickly, hence spending money that would have been better placed in other ways. One of those would have been to grow my used car business first. There is money in used cars, but I didn't focus enough on that aspect of my business, even though it cost me quite a sum of money just to set it up! I had the lot to park them on, and I had the presence on a somewhat busy highway. Clearly, I hadn't thought that through.

When it came down to the bottom line, I also didn't read enough. I didn't gain enough wisdom from others who had ventured into small brick and mortar businesses. Self-development on that topic would have likely served me well. Focus, knowledge, implementation—these are so valuable.

Although I look back and see all the mistakes I made, I also feel proud that I was courageous enough to be a woman and move to a small town and take over an auto repair business. I love every thought of that experience, except the final days when my business closed down. But the lessons I learned were invaluable, and although an expensive way to learn those lessons, I do know that I can build again. This time, I don't plan on the brick and mortar route yet. But with the ambition and persistence I have, I know that the money I lost on that venture will only be a benefit to me in my future ventures.

So no matter if you have tried and failed, and even if it may have cost you money, remember that money is something you can always build upon again. And failing is not an option, because if you take what you learned from the experience, it only means that you are one, or even one thousand, steps closer to your next success.

Implementing Belief And Motivation

Belief. This is something that so many people lack, and particularly as they get older. Life has a way of turning you into a cynic, questioning the truth in everything.

Unfortunately, this *disbelief* also then affects the belief in oneself. Quite often, what your brain is taught reflects on you as well.

Believe me, I understand. I remember wanting to subsidize my income when my auto repair shop was faltering. I had done some minor MLM work previously, and although it seemed that I ended up spending more than I was making, I had not completely lost faith in the possibility of making money with those systems.

Needless to say, it wasn't long before I found myself in the same predicament as I had been in years before. I was spending money with the hope of making money, but the promises these companies made were "pie in the sky" and unachievable. I am sure that there were some out there that were legitimate, but in my case, I seemed to have found the ones that took your money, then shut down, or did not deliver.

I had taken a sabbatical from attempting these ventures, and decided to become an employee for a while. I continued to take courses, pursuing my handwriting certification and my coaching certification, but there was still something missing. I had lost my chance with the free affiliate program that was offered. I signed up, but I was still in hesitation mode. I did not believe; hence, I did not have the motivation to move forward.

Serendipity is one of my favorite words, and like most things in my life that have been worthwhile, they seem to have appeared serendipitously. *(Seeing as the auto correct seems to allow me that last word, I then believe it to be real!)*

It is where I am today. It was by chance that a while ago, I found Handwriting University, and followed my passion to become certified in the field and then complete my master's. What to do with this? I believed in the science; hence, I enjoyed what I was doing, and I was motivated. The University then offered the PRISM Life Design

Coaching certification, which I signed up for, because it did have an element of the handwriting analysis attached to it. Exciting.

However, how was I really going to attain the level of income I really wanted to with this? It all came together when I found, by chance, online, another course that would change the way I was looking at things. The courses were focused on branding yourself.

I put it all together and realized that with my 30 years of marketing experience, and my coaching and my handwriting analysis, I could marry all this together and make it one lucrative business, with "me" as the brand. Brilliant.

What was apparent with all this was that it was real. I believed again, and I found something I could truly put work and effort into, because I could see the future results. There were immediate results, but they were but a glimpse of what I knew could come.

So it is important to find something you believe in. You implement this, and the motivation will come with it. And just imagine yourself being before the people, serving them with what has been served to YOU! It is all up to YOU—now learn how this can become the best reality you have ever imagined.

People Will Buy from You Because of You *(80% Buy if They Like Someone)*

With this comes the first question: Do YOU like yourself? For people to like you, you don't have to really like yourself, but it really helps because there is a genuine aspect involved in exuding your personality.

There is a great saying: "Your smile is your logo, your personality is your business card, and how you make others feel becomes your trademark." I am not sure who wrote that, but those words are priceless.

Let's take one at a time.

Your smile:

This is a universal language and reflects a warmth and invitation to build a relationship. Not everyone, but most people, if you smile at them, will smile back. It is a first impression that can immediately build on the next part.

Your personality:

It is a known fact that if you mimic someone's gestures, they will feel a connection to you. When revealing your personality, be yourself, but also be aware of the person you are with. You may be extremely enthusiastic, and that is wonderful, but if you are in the presence of someone a bit quieter, it serves well to tone down that enthusiasm just a notch. Watch for their hand movements and facial expressions, and let your personality work with that. Understand, however, that you must remain genuine. Don't try too hard. Your smile is the reason they are willing to get to know you a bit better. Your personality is what will entice them to take your business card, or business information.

How you make someone feel:

There is an old adage that states to "treat people the way you want to be treated." As long as you are not a masochist, this holds true. Being kind to someone, serving them, listening to what they have to say, and responding with awareness, are all part of your trademark. Your trademark is what will have people follow you, no matter what product or service you are offering. Your trademark is what develops loyalty and fans.

When you apply these three rules, you are sure to build not just your audience but, as stated before, your loyal fans. This is what you want. When you achieve this, you are sure to be successful 80% of the time in having someone buy from you. Why? Because you have built, with these three pillars, a foundation that inspired your audience to like you, and in so doing, to trust you.

Have you ever gone to a concert where there was an opening band? The reason you went was for the main attraction, right? There are times when that opening band is great, but in truth, you are anticipating watching the group, or singer, that you are a fan of.

When you brand yourself, this is true for you too. People will want to see YOU—not the next person selling or offering the same service.

Go out there and smile, show who you are, and serve.

For proof that this works, continue reading.

Proof It's True, the Best Brand Is YOU

Consider the many people you have heard, seen, followed, and admired out there. I can name many, but then again, it would depend on where you are in life, and what you do. This could be a speaker, a great artist, a writer, an entrepreneur, or a philanthropist.

In all aspects of life, there are the leaders. If you dissect why they are successful in leading, it is apparent that they possess one thing in common: They have branded themselves.

When you associate your name to a cause, a purpose, a product, and you are passionate about it, you are on your way to becoming a leader. You become the "expert"; hence, you are helping to guide others, inspire others, and encourage them to take action.

When you realize that others are inspired by your message, you will find that drive and determination to keep going and to keep serving, and as you do so, your presence will grow.

Let me mention one example that I found inspirational. Years ago, I wanted my children to learn about faith. It wasn't about religion; it was about faith. We "shopped" around for different churches, and I let my children pick the one they were most comfortable with.

We ended up going to a small community gathering of about 100 people. The people there were engaging and non-threatening. I know this last part sounds strange, but if any of you have ever considered attending a place of faith, the first thing you "fear" is a group of overzealous people forcing you into believing what you don't believe, or asking for money, etc.

In this case, there was none of that, and the children truly enjoyed the activities that were available to them. I enjoyed the pastor. Here was this hippy-like guy who had just replaced the previous pastor, who had retired. At the beginning, the congregation watched with suspicion, doubt, excitement, and anticipation. In other words, there were all sorts of feelings going on regarding having a new character up on stage.

This young man, within weeks, had gained the trust and the respect of the people; and fast forward, now has a following of over 6000 people, I believe. A regular service will boast a full movie theatre, which they have now moved into.

Why was he successful in growing his audience and his fans? He doesn't judge; he puts himself in humbling situations; he speaks the truth; he offers a warm, non-threatening atmosphere; he builds enthusiasm; he creates a call to action, and people can relate to him. There is no talk about "religion," only "faith," and people from all walks of life and all kinds of beliefs visit to listen.

Why has he been successful? Humility, passion, honesty, serving others and being himself—all these characteristics are built in to a "brand" per se.

Today, he likely could go out and sell Pet Rocks, and people would likely buy them from him. He has earned that trust.

A little more on how to be "you," and branding yourself, is in the next chapter.

"Science is nothing but perception."
— **Plato**

CHAPTER 2

The Science of YOU
by LAURIEANN

What I Mean by the "Science of YOU" *(Your Energy Is a Science and It Is Contagious)*

People don't see themselves as a "science" per se, but they are. Each individual is filled with energy and a force that makes up their being. That "being" is an element of science, and the main thing here is for you to define your scientific makeup. This is where you gain knowledge of your "self," and get to "know" yourself by splitting out the elements that make you who you are. This is the science of YOU.

What the heck am I talking about? Let me give you an example.

Who are you when you are alone? What are the things you like to do when there is no one around? How do you perceive yourself when you look in the mirror? Where do you go to find peace? When do you feel at your best? Why do you react a certain way to situations?

These are just some of the questions you can ask to define who you are.

Create your own questions. Start with the beginning word, and finish the question. Then answer it.

Who_____?

What_____?

How_____?

Where_____ ?

When_____?

Why_____?

From the questions you asked, and how you answered them, write a paragraph on what you deduced from this exercise. This is the beginning of understanding more about your makeup—your science.

NOTES:

_____

_____

_____

_____

_____

_____

_____

_____

The Basics of the Science of YOU

You, the sum of the parts: parts of your being—your experiences, your actions, and reactions; your emotions, thoughts, physical desires, passions, and dislikes—a map of molecules, sometimes so wrapped up in a web, it creates confusion and overwhelm.

Make a list of positives now:

- Who am I?

- Who do I like?

- What makes me smile?

- What makes me laugh?

- What fills me up?

- What inspires me?

Build yourself around what inspires you about yourself, not what you think others are looking for.

The fact that you are *science* means that you are functioning with all the energy around you. To ensure success, you need to make sure you are focusing on the list above. The positive energy must outdo the negative by a long shot. It takes one small negative to distract you away from the positive. When that negative comes into your life, what you must do is turn your attention toward the list above. Focus on one of the elements. Meditate on it. This will reduce the confusion and overwhelm. Why this chapter? Why are we talking about overwhelm and confusion in branding YOU? It is of the utmost importance, which you will learn in the chapter that follows.

Characteristics That Define You *(To You)*

What are your main characteristics? The previous chapter listed the things that you enjoy. Now we will move on to your characteristics, your traits. We will do this in a different way than you would be used to.

It is an interesting fact that your handwriting is directly connected to the neurons in your brain; hence, your handwriting also will reflect characteristics that even you may not be aware of.

I am offering, in this chapter, a unique opportunity to further learn about these. On my website, www.makeupnotrequired.com, there is a link to submit your handwriting, and I will then send you back a brief list of your main characteristics.

To do so, write with a blue ballpoint pen, on a blank piece of paper, the following:

The crazy purple monkey did not want to go to the zoo. "Why should I go to the zoo?" he asked.

"Because you need to go home," you said to him.

With this, finish off with your signature, and send it along. Remember, the paper has to be blank, and you must use a blue ballpoint pen. Any submission that does not follow these instructions will not receive a response. I say this because accuracy is important, and to be more accurate, these rules must be in place.

Just to let you know, I am a certified handwriting analyst, and have done over 500 handwriting analysis reports. I will also enjoy getting your feedback, which you can do on my website as well, after you receive your short report.

Also on the website, will be the option to get further information about your characteristics, and if desired, a longer report, which can help you to further succeed at your business.

Here are a few further notes in defining yourself to look at:

Acts of kindness

Being born a

_____

Going without, yet

_____

Past challenges conquered

_____

Parents' influence made me

_____

And create your own:

_____

_____

_____

I look forward to engaging with you, and now we can move on to the next chapter.

Moments That Defined You

What were your fondest memories as a child? Was there anything specific that happened to you in your teen years, or recently, that changed your life, changed your mindset, or changed a part of you? Is there something you hold strong to and will not sway?

I know, as a child, I was very exuberant, and I loved to show off, until the age of 3 and a half. At that point, my mother had my sister, and my spotlight as the youngest and the baby of the family was removed. That point in my life changed my character. I became much more of a recluse, and enjoyed my own company much more. I did have friends and enjoyed them, but I also liked being alone. This went on for most of my life. I was shy, ,but once you got to know me, you couldn't shut me up.

As a teen, I was very much into sports and cheerleading. This brought me out of my shell somewhat, in regard to the fear of what others thought, but that fear was still there. It consumed me most of my life.

Anyone relate to these? Are you a middle child? Were you bullied? Were you spoiled and never fearful? Were you fearful but did it anyway?

It's interesting that we all have moments that define us, and those moments are treasures when *branding the true you*, because you are going to be sharing stories about those moments. So, list 10 here to start. We will take this further in a future chapter.

1 _____

2 _____

3 _____

4 _____

5 _____

6 _____

7 _____

8 _____

9 _____

10 _____

What Do You Love Most About "You?"

Noting what you love most about yourself is quite often hard to do. To brand YOU, it is of the utmost importance to find at least a couple of things that you love most about yourself. You will not shine if you don't have that ability to say what it is that you are great at—what makes you look in that mirror in the morning and say, "Let's do this." It takes knowing those parts of you that you love most to get you through tough times too!

Let me give you an example. I have struggled with believing in myself for years. I always thought I was not good enough, or pretty enough, or smart enough. My self-esteem was low for so long. Even married and with children, I still struggled.

Don't get me wrong. I was happy, and I did very well academically because I forced myself to, and I had ambition and always took the road less travelled. I was a literary agent at the age of 24, and even the vice president of the Toronto branch of the Canadian Author's Association, as well as the editor of their newsletter, which I printed on my old computer, a Tandy EX that had no hard drive. I was driven. I joined volunteer groups.

As life progressed, I lost my business by following my husband at the time; but I learned a lot by being his office manager, teaching him about accounting, which made him CFO, and I also did the marketing for 10 years. Then they fired me—conflict of interest.

I turned it around and became the executive director of a not-for-profit that helped people start their own businesses. And here is the story. I went into that interview not really feeling that I deserved to be in that capacity. But what helped was that I was very involved with the Chamber of Commerce, and I was on the board of directors. That got me the career opportunity.

And as great as that felt, and I felt my self-esteem was rising, I was in a relationship that didn't help. It was one where the love of my life wanted me to do well, but then felt I was not doing enough as a mother and a wife.

That relationship ended with great pain, at the same time that I lost my job due to lack of funding.

So I was divorced and bought an auto repair company 4 years later, having been now engaged in the automotive industry. Three years later, the recession happened. But it wasn't all about the recession. It was partially my fault too. In trying to beat the recession, I over-invested in possibilities instead of trying to fix what was bleeding. Not failure but another lesson; but again, I lost the love for myself.

Here is where I found it: when I changed my mindset—when I looked at my achievements rather than the things I didn't manage to make the way I wanted them to be.

Marriages dissolve, businesses dissolve, but the fact that you take a chance on love or business doesn't dissolve. It builds character.

So here, write down the achievements you have in your life (e.g., family, business, volunteering). At the end, I can ensure that you will see that what left your hands never left your heart, or your head, with what you learned from it all.

These are my top 5, but you will write your top 10!! And submit them to our website!

- Author of *Hampy* (created when I was 18; published when I was 48; www.hampy.ca)
- Youngest VP of the Toronto Canadian Authors Association
- First one in my circle of friends to have a sole proprietorship (literary agency) at 24
- Self-employed on the side for 33 years; Pinnacle Award for most volunteering; president of the Chamber of Commerce (not an easy task at 38)
- Adamant about marrying my first true love; together for 22 years, with three children; divorced with no regrets

Your turn:

_____

_____

_____

_____

_____

_____

_____

_____

_____

Putting It All Together

So now that we have these lists, what do we do with them? We are going to build a verbal sketch and an animation sketch of what you look like as a brand.

"What?" you ask.

Well, I know we are not all writers, or artists, but this is not about that. This is an exercise, and it is meant to give you an idea of where you can find your greatest strengths to attract your audience, and the qualities you are most comfortable with that will help you with your brand.

Everyone is different. So, let's start. Once you are done, you are welcome to share this on the website. I would love to see the drawn version of you, or a picture. Let me give you an example below:

A friend of mine said that I am "that handwriting gal." From there, I realized, "I am that gal." From there, I went from a sketch and then to photoshop. And then I thought I could define it better in a picture.

I Am That Gal
Creator of the G.A.L Plan©

It Began as
"The Handwriting Gal"
Then all the Gal parts I
combined through Education and
Experience to create..
The "Get A Life" Plan

LaurieAnn
laurieann@iamthatgal.com

That was the start of "The Handwriting Gal." But then I realized I was more than that, and that I had accomplished so much more. "I Am That Gal," and all that comes with me. So from that, it came to this:

I AM LaurieAnn

Award Winning Handwriting Analyst

You are Unique

Everyone is in their/handwriting

Understand Relationships in business, and in
personal relationships and about YOU and YOUR
successful signature with the Queen of Handwriting

And then this to finally simplify it. I realized this was TOO MUCH.

So I came up with a new picture, but with a constant.

Just to let you know what the dictionary states about the science of you, here are two versions:

Webster's Dictionary defines science as the state of knowing: knowledge as distinguished from ignorance or misunderstanding.

(History and Etymology for Science –

Middle English, from Anglo-French, from Latin scientia, from sciens (scientis), having knowledge, from present participle of scire "to know"; perhaps akin to Sanskrit chyatihe, cuts off; Latin scindere to split, shed.)

CHAPTER 3

The Fire in YOU
by Robert Max Wall

What Is the Spark That You Want to Ignite? *(No Pyromaniacs Allowed)*

So let's talk about *purpose*, the *reason* behind creating and defining this YOU-brand. But first, let me introduce myself. It is my honor to co-author alongside this amazing woman, LaurieAnn Campbell; so much in fact that when she asked if I would like to collaborate with her on this journey, it was an absolute no-brainer.

I was born a few moons ago as Robert Max Wall, in the happening town of Kalamazoo, Michigan... YES, there really is a Kalamazoo. My family has a very rich history in that area, but I'll save that for another chapter that better defines how DNA can contribute to your makeup as well. So, back to that "spark." As you continue this journey toward branding YOU, in order to truly be successful at whatever you're called to do, you must spend some time determining whom you'd like to serve, and what your higher purpose is, above the simplistic thought of just earning a living.

The best way I can define this, based on the overall premise of this book, is to take another hard look at the definition of branding: *"the action of marking or placing a mark...."* So, what mark do you want to leave on this world? Rather than imagining this as a figurative mark with a branding iron, think of it as an impression you plan to leave on the hearts, minds, and lives of many.

You may already know this answer, but whether you have or have not defined your purpose, this exercise will help narrow down your thoughts to truly understand *the spark you'd like to ignite.*

1. What is your passion? Think of a time when you felt a sense of meaning in your life, business, or career.

2. Who were/are you serving? One of the most powerful life-drivers can be found in your service to others.

3. What impact did/do you have on others in serving this purpose? How were they able to benefit?

Friction Generates Heat, So Keep That Fire Burning

Now that you have explored and possibly discovered your TRUE purpose, how do you reignite that spark and keep that fire burning? We know, similar to rubbing your hands together, friction causes molecules to move faster, providing more energy. This creates a higher temperature, resulting in warmth and heat.

We also know that other elements come into play. It's a fact that the rougher the surface and the greater the weight, the more friction comes into play. So let's assume that this analogy applies to the mind and heart. If your thoughts and your path toward a greater self, a better YOU, were smooth and trouble-free, how would you generate enough fortitude to overcome obstacles in life?

In Robert Frost's poem, "The Road Not Taken," he mentions that "...Two roads diverged in a wood, and I took the one less traveled by, and that has made all the difference." This mindset reinforces that by avoiding all pain and all obstacles, we will never learn. We need these frictions in our lives, in order to generate enough heat to ignite that fire deep inside us. When your *passion* is ignited by your *purpose*, you are unstoppable.

Are you still questioning your own abilities? Do you find yourself doubting this stride toward victory? Whether big or small, rich or poor, fast or slow, you have the ability to created greatness. Sticking with my theme of friction and heat, did you know that a single candle can generate immense heat? The inner core of a candle flame is light blue, with a temperature of approximately 1,500° Celsius, or 2,732° Fahrenheit... YOU don't have to be a rampid forest fire to generate heat.

Visualize yourself as a candle, which not only generates an immense amount of heat from its core, but also provides light, revealing dangers along your path less traveled. Remember that your spark, your heat, and your light are not only elements for your own greatness, but by revealing this power within, others around you will benefit as well. We will be discussing the importance of "sharing the fire," in the next section.

So, now that we've explored your WHY, your true purpose, and defined that friction is the catalyst to heat, in building that fire from within, let's explore how to keep that fire burning.

Have you heard the term, "Keep or stay around the campfire?" This concept, which I discuss deeper in my course, "Bonfire Tribe," explains that our activities around the campfire are not only informative but essential in our service to others. When you huddle together around the fire, which provides warmth and security, you start to build a stronger desire and clarity around community. It is in this moment that you are able to share and, in turn, grow from this wealth of information being shared by others who are experiencing your same pain, or have triumphed over it. Gathering around the fire puts relationships and human needs at the center of your purpose, resulting in a campfire that continues to grow. The larger the campfire, the more contributors you'll attract. This increased contribution will ensure effectiveness in keeping that fire burning inside YOU and the others around you.

Sharing the Fire – Igniting the Purpose for Others

Now that you're aware of the "campfire" or "bonfire" concept, ask yourself this: How can my service toward others help in my life, relationships, career, or business? First off, serving is addictive and transferable. Serving others is in our DNA from birth. The simple act of helping and serving someone else, releases hormones like oxytocin, the same chemical that helps us fall deeply in love with others and ourselves. This also helps build trust in building strong relationships, and in business interactions, which is why people innately buy from those they "know, like, and trust."

Let's break this down into 4 key points, with famous quotes to back this mindset.

1.   "No one has ever become poor by giving." ~Anne Frank

a. Create value. Solve another person's pain, and you will receive back all of the ingredients required toward creating success: joy, love, wisdom, experience, perspective, gratitude, happiness, just to name a few.

b. What can/do you offer to others? Think of ways you can give of your talents, your time, and your financial blessings.

2. "The happiest people are not those getting more, but those giving more." ~H. Jackson Brown Jr.

a. We've already discovered that you'll receive more by serving others, but what's the point of it all unless you are truly happy. Happiness instills creativity, confidence, passion, and fulfillment.

b. Make a list of the things you've accomplished in life, relationships, and business. What was your mood in these moments? This exercise will help you tap into your passion and purpose.

3. "He who serves the most, reaps the most." ~Robin Sharma

a. A healthy mind leads to a healthy body. Science, and the results from successful people, reinforces this. This is all connected in the ecosystem of mindset. So, if serving creates happiness, and happiness improves health, resulting in more productivity, then success becomes just one step closer.

b. Volunteering can help YOU live longer! A person's will to LIVE, correlates directly with having something to live for. *SUCCESS* magazine states that those who volunteer more than 100 hours per year, are only one-third as likely to die, and have overall health. That's only 2 hours per week! Are you currently operating at optimal performance in mind, heart, and health?

List a few ways in which you would be able to serve your community or mankind.

4. "You can have everything you want, if you will just help other people get what they want." ~Zig Ziglar

    a. We've explored the mindset and heartset required to gain more financial control over your life by serving others. If you can achieve all of this by gaining a healthier lifestyle and having a great BIG smile on your face, would you go ALL IN?

    b. Serving others improves your relationships. Create a list of the 5 people that you've impacted positively in life. Reach back out to them and ask, "How can I serve you and your mission in a greater way?" This will not only solidify the relationship you already have with them, but potentially open up the door for further opportunity. Additionally, create a list of 5 people you'd like to serve; reach out to them by introducing yourself and letting them know your intentions of building stronger relationships (no sales pitch), and then ask the simple question: "How am I able to serve you, and what other connections are you looking for?" Helping others with their pain, equips us with the tools necessary in managing our own challenges in life, relationships, and business.

Igniting Others

Some ideas of how to ignite others:

-   Webinars
-   Going Live or using a platform like ZOOM
-   Presentations – Print, Video or Audio
-   Keep in contact with your Tribe across all social media platforms

Remember… Feedback helps with knowing how to better serve and pass on your "Torch of Passion" to others.

*"Sending a handwritten letter is becoming such an anomaly. It's disappearing. My mom is the only one who still writes me letters. And there's something visceral about opening a letter—I see her on the page. **I see her in her handwriting.**"*
— **Steve Carrell**

CHAPTER 4

Building the YOU-Esteem
by LAURIEANN

Write This and Analyze It

Ever since I was 9 years old, I have been intrigued with handwriting analysis. Some of you may start reading this paragraph with an "oh-oh," and some with awe, some with trepidation, and some with curiosity; but it is something I always wanted to know more about. I found my wonder in it through books, and then by graduating, at 52, as a certified handwriting analyst.

Great. I have the certificate. But I don't have the self-esteem to believe enough that I can make others understand that this is a real science. Why not? Fear of ridicule, fear of failure? Partially. But perhaps the biggest issues have been my six points listed below.

Knowing yourself—what compels you, what motivates you, and even the opposite, what slows you down—is important. Let's take the latter for a moment. It is important to know yourself in order to control what slows you down. Some of the points, I have placed below; and these emotions will lower the building blocks of your self-esteem.

- Disruption (social media; too many requests for help, and wanting to, but time… time…)
- Lack of focus (What is my direction?)
- Anxiety (Can I do all this? In other words, being organized.)
- External forces (e.g., working toward your dream but still employed)

- Energy (overwhelm, being sick but not giving up, family issues, then not showing up)
- Feeling incompetent (Again, this may come from an external source, such as your job, not from your ambition.)

Please write yours here, and feel free to share them on our website.

_____

_____

_____

_____

_____

_____

_____

_____

_____

_____

_____

_____

Life-Changing Activity (*Emotional Appraisal of Our Own Worth*)

When this book was first started, we were in a "normal" kind of time. But recently, there has been a pandemic, and COVID-19 has changed people's lives, including their perceptions; and for me, this has been exactly what this chapter is about.

I incorporated into my life many life-changing activities that were not really *placed upon me*—but in a sense, they were. I had four weeks of isolation, so to speak, and in that time, it provided me with the insightfulness to appraise my own worth. And it was an emotional time.

To move forward to brand my "YOU," I had to focus on what was stopping me throughout my life. In order to move forward with YOUR brand, it is very important to know WHO you are and what you need to do to change aspects of your life that may be holding you back.

One of the things I decided I would start doing was to actually write cards and letters, and go back to feeding other people's mailboxes. Not the virtual kind, and not typed letters—handwritten, and sealed with a wax stamp. What created this change in mindset while in isolation? The realization that everyone needs a sense of PURPOSE. What life-changing activity can you do to give yourself a sense of PURPOSE?

This step is so simple. It doesn't need to be a grandiose step in your life to give you that sense. You don't need to save a village or climb a mountain. It can be as simple as taking the time to pull out a pen and paper, writing something, and then putting that thought in an envelope, and finding a stamp, then walking to the mailbox, and putting the envelope in there. And at the other end, at that address, there will be someone most likely incredibly surprised that you took the time. What was that PURPOSE? A simple one: to make someone smile.

When we are branding ourselves, it is really important to understand even the smallest "life-changing activities" that are not so small to others.

When was the last time you received a truly personalized card or letter in the mail? When was the last time your client received the same?

To the emotional appraisal of your own worth, this is a part of that. What is your worth? It is not all about money or what you own; your integrity and ability to be honest and to provide your client with the best experience ever, is what your worth should be based on. And that "worth" needs to be YOU and your brand.

I truly believe that since the COVID-19 pandemic, reaching out genuinely in ways previously used, which died in our present world of technology, will become even more important. Personal relationships between YOU and your clients will be even more important than ever, online or in person.

Find your life-changing activity. Find something that makes YOU who YOU are, and which makes YOU unique. Is it a letter in the mail? Is it a "just because" card or phone call? Is it providing a "thumper" experience to your client instead of sending online PDFs? Is it surprising them with a nice little token of your appreciation?

I do have to say that the most wonderful experience was a bouquet of flowers that was sent to me when I signed up for a mentorship program. Yes, I am a woman, and believe it or not, not the biggest fan of flowers, because they die. But in this case, it was so lovely that I dried all the flowers and made them into an everlasting memory of the gesture. That, to me, was a life-changing activity from my group, and to my community that I have been involved with for 12 years, and my family.

A great thought with the next one: What life-changing experience can YOU provide, as your brand, to your clients?

Small life-changing experiences provide you with a purpose and with worth; and it is true. We are all selfish, but if being "selfish" is your needing to feel good about helping others, that is the best kind of "selfish" you can be. If everyone on this earth was that kind of "selfish," what a great world it would be.

Keep opening your eyes to new opportunities to change your life's activities, and keep an eye on your emotional appraisal of your worth, through following the path of PURPOSE. If your purpose is not something that at the end of the day doesn't serve you or others, then it's a good idea to re-evaluate it.

Write down 5 life-changing activities that come to mind:

_____

_____

_____

_____

Write down 5 things that you can think of that would give you a PURPOSE (try to write at least 3 simple ones):

_____

_____

_____

_____

_____

Now write down how you feel these can be implemented in YOUR brand:

_____

_____

_____

_____

_____

Learning to Know and Grow *(Growing Through Personally Building Your Education)*

I love this topic, KNOW AND GROW. We never "know" everything, but we can "grow" from knowing more. As a lifetime learner, this is a passionate part of my life.

Now, I have been told that you have to read, read, read. I have to admit, I go through trends of reading avidly, and then I just don't want to pick up a book. But I will say that even during the times that a book is not opened, there is always a new course I have open on my computer, or a new online webinar, or interactive ZOOM session. I never stop.

I also am an avid techy. I have been on computers since they first came out. I know, I am aging myself, but I seriously started on a Commodore 64, and then went to a Tandy EX, which had no hard drive. I also started on a 300 baud, and was so excited to reach people on BBS systems across the world. I am so excited that I lived through the beginning of all this technology. It was even fun being an online private investigator, because it was so easy to catch people way back then. That was all fun, but my point is, I taught myself all that I knew about technology, through research and putting it into practice.

Research and put it into practice—yes, practice—because we have to do a lot of that before we get it right.

How do you start? First of all, if you are passionate about what you do, you start to Google courses and such, to find that one perfect course, or that one perfect book to help. Guess what happens?

Well, back in the early 1990s, this would have been an easier task. Today? You are inundated with so many offers, courses, free this, free that, "I" promises...endless overwhelm.

Where do you start? Some like to follow the most popular people in the world: the Tony Robbins's, the Gary V's, the Shark Tank people, and in Canada, where it started, the Dragon Den successes. There is nothing wrong with that. They are out there, and their names are popular. It is quite funny, though, that in my life, my daughter introduced me to Ray Dalio, and there are so many people I speak to who have never heard of him. Yet he is one of the richest people on earth. You know the owner of Tesla, but you don't know Ray.

Moving forward, there are also successful people you haven't heard of, who have been my mentors. They may not be as rich as the ones stated above, but they are rich in knowledge, and in reaching out and building a true community that is a family.

When I first started on my journey of learning, I did reach out to Tony Robbins. But then along the way, I found Bart Baggett and Raymond Aaron. Along with meeting Bart, I found Dave Grayson. These are names you may not know, but they are my mentors and successful people.

I find their success appealing to me. I know we speak to our fear of success. I believe we fear failure more than success. I learned through my mentors that not trying means you will never fail, and that is a comfortable spot. Not asking for what you are worth is another comfortable spot. Neither of those situations, however, will lead to your success. Neither is thinking that you have to be in a place where name dropping your heroes makes you better than finding less popular heroes, who have one-on-one time for you when you need it.

My point here is to *learn*. But along the way, don't discount some incredible people you can learn from. They don't need to be in the top spotlight list. They may be under a different spotlight. And when you find your "mentors," I recommend you stay with them. You may have one or two. (I don't recommend more than two; it becomes an overwhelm.) You may read about as many successful people as you want, but when you decide your path, and you want to achieve success, pick no more than two mentors to follow.

Learning can be overwhelming at its best these days. As long as you know your path, your passion, and what you want to do, you will find the right balance and the right groups to connect with. Just make sure, on your journey, NOT to overwhelm. It is really important to BALANCE.

I would like you to make a list of four top mentors in your life. Then below, I would like you to research four more mentors that are in a different "spotlight." People tend to gravitate toward the very top, but there is a group of very successful people that are at the "top" of your industry or what you provide as a service; and the spotlight is not as bright, but they are brighter than the spotlight.

FOUR MENTORS THAT TOP RANKED MEDIA PERSONALITIES

_____

_____

_____

_____

FOUR MENTORS THAT ARE SUCCESSFUL IN YOUR INDUSTRY

_____

_____

_____

_____

Now I would like you to write the benefits of engaging with your media personalities versus your successful mentors in your industry. Mine would be quite short and sweet: the price point, the attentiveness, the ability to be a part of a true community that connects and shares on a smaller scope, but more meaningful; versus being costly and a part of an ocean, regardless of what I learn. There is not that connection with spotlight mentors, like I get from my successful mentors, who do not have to be in the limelight all the time.

YOUR TURN:

_____

_____

_____

_____

_____

_____

_____

_____

_____

_____

_____

YOUR learning to define "YOU," through education and learning about who you are, takes time to achieve. It also takes opening your eyes to opportunities to learn from amazing people around you as well. Reach out, join a group, join a mastermind—but remember: Don't overdo it, because if YOU get lost in all the other people's identities and brands, YOU won't define yourself. Learn and practice, but make sure YOU define YOUrself in the process. Be YOU. Not someone else.

It IS About the People *(Who You Hang Around With)*

It *is* about "the people"—the ones you hang around with; the ones you find as mentors; the ones you find as friends.

I recently saw a wonderful post that stated that there are those that spiral downward, and those that spiral upward.

What would you prefer? The image on the next page is quite compelling.

Now, to that image, there is something to be said for someone who generally spirals upward, than being in contact with a "downward spiraling" character. When the two get intertwined, it can cause the "upward spiraling" character to feel anxiety and lose focus.

This is the reason you must create an environment that secures your continual upward movement.

I remember when I was running a not-for-profit, which was a program to help people on government assistance to start their own businesses. We valued the positive aspect of doing so, all the while making sure that there was an understanding that self-employment and entrepreneurship were not easy or simple paths to follow. We had to make sure that they understood that there were going to be difficult times and challenges, and possible failures. (Granted, we never used the "f" word. We preferred to refer to it as congratulatory attempts.)

This was one of the most fulfilling "jobs" I ever had. I coached over 100 start-up businesses during that period, and we had an 82% success rate of businesses still running after the initial difficult three years, and an unprecedented percentage of successes that surpassed the first three years.

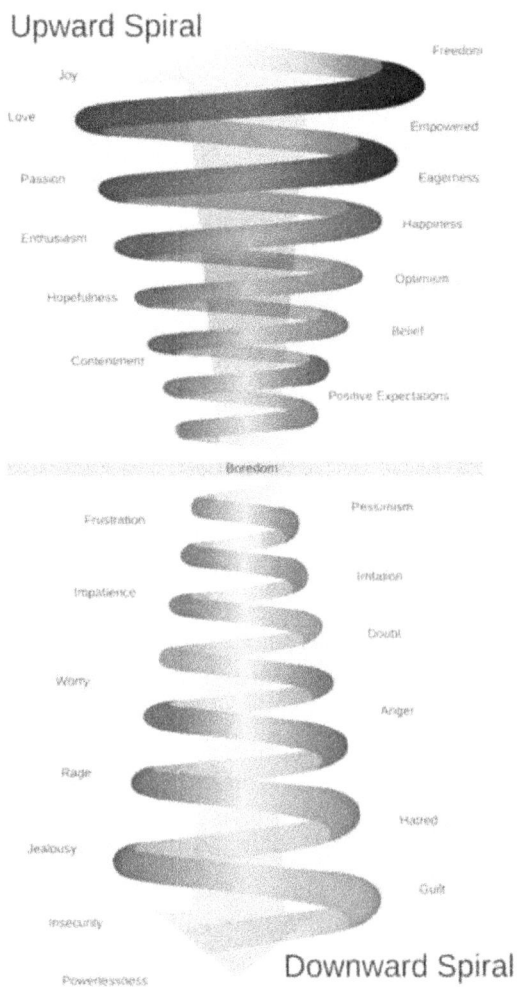

So, where am I going with this? We built a positive, upward spiraling community.

The ironic thing was that even with all my enthusiasm, the building of a community with an alumnus and membership, advocating for a 50% discount to our "students" for Chamber and Board of Trades across the 6 communities we represented, managing to connect my "students/clients" with over $1,000,000 worth of contracts through my contacts, building an interactive website to promote not only our organization but also our students, working overtime with volunteer time, and creating several fundraising events annually, including an exclusive "Dine with the CEO" contest, which included some of the top Canadian entrepreneurs, it remained that when I met with the board of directors, I was not doing enough. Here is my point. It was not all ten members of the board of directors that I reported to that had this opinion. It was ONE downward spiraling personality that no one wanted to stand up to. The board was made up of ten volunteers. As a non-paid board, they did not want conflict; and they did not want to stand up to that one negative element. They just sat and listened as he put me down for the minutest thing and never recognized my achievements. He brought everyone else down with him—he managed to intertwine his negative spiraling with the upward spiraling of nine other members. It silenced my positive group, and made for a very sad scenario.

I experienced this, too, as a volunteer board member and a volunteer president of an organization. There is always one. There was one when I was president, who would have liked nothing more than to see me voted out. But in this case, I actually reached out to my positive-spiraling advocates, and when it came to standing up to her, she ended up quitting. But it doesn't always end with a happy story like that one. However, the moral of that story was that I did take action to pull together the positive team, and say, "Enough is enough – I need backup!" Negative people can be very powerful. Quite often, you need a team of at least four, to go up against one. It is a strange thing, but it is reality.

The recap is that for most people, it takes one downward-spiraling character in your life to disturb the peace and cause a very uncomfortable intertwine.

Hence, to the topic of this chapter, it is important to make sure that if you can avoid a downward spiral, then do so. If you cannot, then make sure that there is someone you can connect with to discuss the situation and the frustration, and to keep you going upwards to release you of that intertwine. If it means that you have to quit an organization that has one of those, or to fire someone or terminate your contract with them, then do it. Those people are never an asset, to your company or your mindset.

So here I want you to think about anyone in your life that may be a downward-spiraling person while you are focused on being an upward-spiraling person. Take stock. You must recognize them. Now, if it is a situation where you cannot terminate or remove that person, your next task is to write down who you can reach out to, to help you when those people are affecting your life.

Downward-spiraling person   Upward-spiraling person

_____

_____

_____

_____

_____

_____

_____

Your Inner Voices *(Choose to Listen to the Right One)*

Now, this is a really good but scary thought: trusting YOUR inner voice.

There are many times in our lives that we have choices to make. We reach that "fork in the road," and we have to choose which way we will go.

My experience is that I have taken the "road less traveled" on many occasions, and I can tell you that it was not always the "right" choice, but in the end, it was.

This may sound contradictory, but I even believe that the road I took that led me to lose my life savings, also brought me to a place where I needed to be, here and now.

I have to be honest. The night of my wedding rehearsal, my gut was saying, "Don't do it." I didn't have the "guts" to walk away.

Then, at the beginning of my marriage, one year into it, I was advised by my husband that he had a post in Reno, Nevada—a bit of a distance from Toronto, Canada. I had also been working hard for three years on building my literary agency. I had made the deal that I would be more than willing to follow him, as long as I could take my business with me. He made a promise that it would be just fine to do that. It ended up that it was a false promise, and I lost my business.

So, what was the good in that? If I had not gone, it may well have ended up in a quick divorce, and I would not have had the opportunity to experience the most unconditional love anyone can have, as the mother of my son that was born while in Reno. I would not have been so frustrated as to not move to another exciting experience of a sideline business designing clothes, and taking that back with me to Canada when we moved back three years later. I might not have had the opportunity to hone my skills in accounting and marketing, which has been a very big part of my life in the past 30 years. I would not have continued with my marriage to see the birth of my beautiful daughter and youngest son. I would have missed out on so much that is precious to me today.

As much as I questioned my choice for quite a few years, today, I do not at all.

Was the choice made from my inner voice? I am not sure. Doubt can conflict with the right decisions. But it did make me stronger. I remember writing to the Senator of Nevada, Richard Bryan, asking for assistance to keep my literary agency going, and I even sent one to Ronald Regan, then President of the United States. Believe it or not, I received a letter from Richard Bryan, stating that he had tried to find a solution but was not successful. And I also received a reply from one of Ronald Regan's assistants, saying the same thing. That was how determined I was.

I love the saying that Raymond Aaron has; that my downfalls were just "a marketing lesson."

Like Raymond, 22 years after meeting my first love, and 15 years after marrying him, my marriage failed, in the same month that I was laid off from one of the most satisfying careers I have ever experienced.

My marketing experience was not complete yet though. Four years after a grueling divorce settlement agreement, and after ending up selling cars as a job, then becoming a service advisor at an independent auto repair shop, I decided I was going to buy my own shop. My research was quite intensive, and my business plan was over 100 pages. I believed that buying an existing business was the better way to go, one that showed steady income and growth. The town had great expansion plans. I visited the location and felt good about it, but my gut was not in it 100%—only my head. I had my favorite mentor, my father, come out to take a look, as well as my then-boyfriend, who had been in the auto body business for years. I felt that they could talk me out of it if they felt that it was not a good idea. I went forth with their blessing, but in hindsight (2020), I had this feeling in the pit of my stomach that the seller was not forthright.

One year into the business, the one employee who had been with him, admitted that the books had been "fudged," and that the previous owner had been losing money.

Now I could say that it would have been a better choice to follow my gut instinct, and in this case, this is partially true when it comes to the loss of everything I had financially. However, I have to look at the positives that came from this experience; the marketing experience. What were they?

The fun part was that I very much enjoyed my three years, running not only a business but a hobby farm with chickens, a donkey, two goats, seven dogs and cats, and a chinchilla.

The hard-knocks lesson was that the loss of my business was not just because of the economy. It was also because I had panicked and expanded the business, putting us in jeopardy with cash flow. I also failed to focus on the money-making aspect, which was a very expensive investment I had made to add a used car dealership to the business.

I was reading Anik Singal's book, *eSCAPE*, and a very strong message to me was that you have to take responsibility for your business failures, or you are not going to succeed the next time. Finger pointing will not make you a stronger person or more resilient or wiser. You need to take stock and accountability. It took me almost ten years to do that. And when I finally did, I felt a sense of freedom.

I did this with my marriage as well. I started taking responsibility for my actions there as well.

All in all, I can look back fondly on it. It didn't end up a bad time in my life because, as earlier said, I believe you go through things that take you to where you need to be. And having lost most of my material possessions (went from a 2400-square-foot home, to a 900-square-foot apartment), it opened my eyes to how rich I was in love and support from family and friends.

During my time running my business, I also found Handwriting University, and published a book I had written when I was 22, about a character that I created when I was 18. On Hampy's 30th anniversary, he became a published book. I still own the 100 submissions to publishers when I was 22, and keep them with pride. Then our progress in technology allowed me to self-publish, and he is now on Amazon!

I am also now a certified handwriting analyst and grapho therapist, and am soon to be a holder of a master's in handwriting analysis certification. I completed the PRISM Life Design coaching course, am an authorized mentor for Handwriting University International, and am founder of the I Am That GAL© Plan.

It has been a journey that created MY BRAND.

All these were seeds that were planted during the time when I was also going through a very tough challenge of running a brick and mortar business.

And these are the things that I feel in my gut to be right for me. Now, on the marketing side, I have the experience and can share with people what to do and what not to do, with my experience in business and relationships. I have the experience to market the knowledge that I have consumed through my journey.

This brings me to the next "listen to your inner voice."

I recommend that you listen to it, but it is not always right, in the sense that if there is something you are passionate about, don't confuse "doubt" with "gut" feelings. Is there a perfect equation or scientific answer to knowing the difference? Not at all.

So how do you choose the right one? I always like the old way: a pros and cons list. And when you are doing this, don't forget to add the possibilities of acts of God, recessions, and worst-case scenarios, along with the best-case scenarios. I say this because, quite often, new entrepreneurs will look more toward the roses than the thorns. And again, is this a guarantee you will make that right choice? Nothing ever is, but regardless, remember to enjoy the experience!! It is just another part of your life that is building YOU and YOUR brand.

What are you wanting to do? What are your pros and cons? And remember to include how your business will best brand YOU.

PROS   CONS

_____   _____

_____   _____

_____   _____

_____   _____

_____   _____

_____   _____

_____   _____

_____   _____

_____   _____

You Are the Authority *(of YOU, So Don't Bully Yourself)*

I LOVE THIS SUBJECT. Yes, I capitalized that, because this subject was what my first book, Hampy, was all about. It is one thing for others to bully you, but your worst enemy, sometimes, is YOU!

The strangest thing happened to me today as I was ready to write about this subject. My sister texted me. Our conversation went on to my son, who disowned me as a mother five months ago. She told me that he had said to her back then, after he had sent me a very nasty message, which I cannot share, that he didn't "respect" me. I thought about that for quite some time. I was also hurt by the verbal gun that my sister shot at me, and I shot back. Again, I don't want to bring this to this table, but my day was destroyed for completing anything I wanted to get done. I was an emotional wreck.

Then I reached out to a friend, a new family friend, as I see him, and he told me that I did not create this mess. People create their own. I am paraphrasing, but it made sense.

I could have looked upon this exactly how he saw it. "Let them say what they want, but how do you feel about yourself?" Truly, I know I haven't been the perfect person, but I do feel good about myself. Yet I spent the whole day second-guessing myself again, after years of learning how not to!

"You are the authority of YOU!" STOP bullying yourself. Bullying yourself can easily come from the most minute moment in your life, when that ONE word may take you back to recap things that YOU never had control over, or even if you did, you didn't quite know how at the time. Why? Because YOU are HUMAN.

It's another list. Take inventory of the things YOU did so well, and that you were proud of, no matter how small, versus the things people tell you about YOU, which you ponder to the point that YOU are the one that is bullying YOURSELF.

Take deep breaths, then make a list of your kindest and dearest friends to reach out to. Why? Because when you make that list, you will realize that if you need to, you have someone there.

What if you don't? My daughter complains about this all the time, that she doesn't have friends.

Friends are found. Then true friendships are made through time, through relating.

Some come and some may go. Some may come back years later. The ones that come back with open arms, you reach right back. But there is a reason to reach back. They are the ones that meant a great deal and made your life wonderful when you were with them, and you just simply lost touch. They aren't the ones that chose to close you out. Those who did, think hard before taking them back. There might have been a very good reason why they closed you out, and you may not want to revisit that. You may just rehash your self-bullying. They are not your future. They are your past. Leave them there.

To stop "bullying' yourself, you have to make sure that the people and friends around you are on the same page. They are the ones that lift you, not knock you down. They are the ones that when they were down, you did the same. They are the ones that you can talk to, and when you do, you know they were always there, even when they weren't. They were and are the spirit you uphold by remembering those amazing times, and by remembering the ones they created, the ones they are creating today, and the ones they are yet to create. They are the ones that never took advantage of YOU but of your strengths, because it made them better; and the ones YOU took advantage of, learning from THEIR strengths, not THEM, to make YOU a better person, and that wonderful bond continues.

Your "authority of YOU" comes in the believing that you are always in the inertia stage, and that you can choose who is around you. It's creating your aura. It's a secret to branding YOU. It's your ability to stop bullying yourself, and to make sure that those in your circle are rocks, and the foundation that keeps you grounded.

Shine, and believe in YOU. Don't bully the most important person in your life—YOU.

This is not an ego comment. Most people don't realize it, but when it comes down to it, you are the only one in this life that will wake up with you, be there for you, live with you, and die with you. That last part may sound a bit morbid, but think about it; it's true! So make sure you are kind to yourself. Make sure, along with all the great people you choose to have around you, YOU are one of them.

Here is your inventory. I took the deliberation of starting with the most important for you. 😊

WHO I WANT IN MY LIFE   WHO IS BETTER NOT IN MY LIFE

_____   _____

_____   _____

_____   _____

_____   _____

_____   _____

_____   _____

Incidentally, the very first book I wrote, at 22, about my cartoon character, Hampy, which I created when I was 18, was about this subject. Again, as I am noting this, I was about to write, "It's not the best book," and then I had to think back and say to myself, "I am so proud of this book! It's not one of the top-100 *New York Times* bestsellers, but I wrote it and illustrated it at 22! And it is published and now on AMAZON." Take note of how you speak about YOUrself. Turn the bully into a cheerleader inside of yourself. And DON'T let any thoughts come into your mind and ruin any celebration. Show those thoughts to the door. ☺

"A person who never made a mistake never tried anything new."
– Albert Einstein

CHAPTER 5

Creating a Confident YOU
Identify YOU, Boost Your Confidence,
and Step Away From Comfort
by Robert Max Wall

Does Confidence Differ from Esteem?

Quite often, people conflate confidence and esteem together. In the previous chapter, LaurieAnn helped us outline esteem. Esteem, plain and simple, is our own sense of self. Confidence, however, is a measure of faith in one's own abilities. Combined, both our thoughts and emotions influence how we perceive others and interact with this world.

Although both confidence and esteem complement each other well, they don't always go hand in hand. The biggest mistake I see by conflating one with the other, is in the outcome of these results. Most end up with a list of achievements and accolades, rather than a constructive list displaying areas for improvement. Although satisfactory for others, a longer list of certificates, diplomas, or acknowledgments does not necessarily equate to better self-esteem. In many cases, this long list of accomplishments only masks this empty desire for status, relationships, or wealth.

So how do we change our mindset around this? If confidence means to trust, and self-confidence to trust in oneself, then it's imperative to believe in your own abilities. Many struggle with this core practice of believing in YOU. A good friend, Les Brown, said something that has resonated with me for many years. Les said, "If you lack confidence, first find someone else who believes in you while you're learning to believe in yourself." You see, someone needs to be your biggest fan, way before you experience this yourself. This is why I encourage you to always be coachable, and to find yourself a mentor. Additionally, as we've learned, when you are in service to others, you become someone else's champion, resulting in a solid foundation for building self-confidence.

Improvement Starts with YOU

Guess what? YOU are uniquely made, and even some of these challenges you face are unique. However, this journey of becoming your best, most-confident self, does not have to be unique or treated as an unchartered land of trials and tribulations. There are tips, tricks, and tools available to help you cope with these challenges. This poses true for almost every barrier that prevents you from reaching your goals of confidence and esteem.

If improvement first starts with YOU, then it's important to understand the difference between *force* and *focus*. Forcing yourself to make changes, will more than likely end in defeat, but focusing on the result of these changes, tapping into a motivation from deep within, can make the difference. You are one step closer to experiencing true transformation.

Here are a few ways you can boost self-confidence and reprogram the mindset of the past.

1. Affirmation of Self (*The Success Principles*, by Jack Canfield)

    - Start with the words, "I am."
    - Focus on the present tense.
    - State it in the positive. What do you want?
    - Keep it brief and specific.
    - Include an action word ending with "ing."
    - Describe at least one dynamic emotion or feeling.
    - Make affirmations for "self," not others.

Example: *"I am so happy and grateful that I am now celebrating having achieved my ideal weight of 140 pounds."*

2. Visualize Your Best Self – The Perfect YOU

   - Look into the future (1–5 years), and imagine your best self.
   - Imagine, with vivid detail, all you have accomplished in life.
   - Now make a list. If it doesn't make you smile, it's not for you.
   - Provide character strength details from your observation.
   - Most importantly, what character strengths and actions are required to now make this a reality?

   Note: You can reverse these steps by creating the image first.

3. Serve Others

   - Change your position. You can serve and lead well, by taking on the role of the servant. Leave your personal agenda behind.
   - Take time to truly listen, honoring their opinions and sharing their pain.
   - Care at any cost. Asking, "How may I help you," opens up the possibility of an answer that may change your personal schedule or agenda.
   - Be open to the idea that you may not be the only solution.

   To serve well, have faith that you are ultimately serving someone greater than SELF.

4. Socialize

   - Put yourself out there (stores, coffee shops, outdoor events).
   - Take action over avoiding interaction.
   - Avoid isolation.
   - If face-to-face is too much now, look into virtual meetups, or

search for Facebook groups that align with your interests.
- Volunteering helps build social skills, esteem, and confidence.

5. Develop a Tribe (Bonfire)

- Build your tribe around those who champion and uplift you.
- Your tribe can help you find SELF, during discovery.
- Select your members around a common goal or interest.
- Leverage social media to find like-minded individuals.
- Start a blog or podcast to vet your tribe and fan the campfire.
- Collaborate on projects with others, and build joint ventures.
- SERVE. Helping others get what they want, builds your tribe.
- Look for and utilize the 1/3 Rule of Attraction... 1/3 of those you come across will dislike you (usually for no reason); 1/3 will be indifferent toward you; and 1/3 will LOVE YOU and will agree to ignore the first 2/3rds!

"One of the most fundamental human needs is the need to belong." Noted psychologist, Abraham Maslow, identified it as one of the five basic needs.

6. Do One Thing That Scares You Every Day (Face Your Fears)

- Act, regardless of the negative voices in your head!
- Be prepared for discomfort. Getting comfortable with being uncomfortable is where transformation begins.
- Begin to step outside of your comfort zone.
- Create challenges and seek an accountability partner.

7. Take a Rejection Challenge

The purpose is to desensitize yourself from the pain of rejection, and to overcome fear. Make it ethical, legal, and physically possible. (Concept from "100 Days of Rejection Therapy" ~ Jia Jiang)

- Request a refill of your food at a fast food restaurant.
- Speak over the intercom in any store.
- Borrow $50 from a stranger.
- Ask to cut in line multiple times on Black Friday or Boxing Day.
- Give $5 to five random people.
- Become a live mannequin at a store.
- Ask a stranger for a compliment.
- Welcome people at your favorite restaurant.
- Challenge your superior to a staring contest.
- Offer to pump someone's gas at a station.

...and so on. You get the idea. Have fun creating this list!

Complete a SWOT Analysis on Self

Sometimes the answer is already inside YOU. One other great exercise in building better self-confidence, is to perform a SWOT analysis on yourself.

If you are unfamiliar with this concept, SWOT stands for: **S**trengths, **W**eaknesses, **O**pportunities, and **T**hreats.

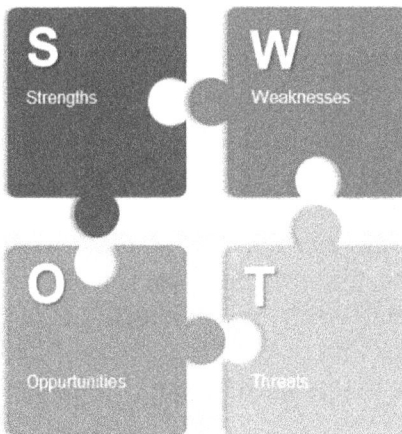

This method of analyzing was originally created over 50 years ago. SWOT was developed initially to be used on complex projects or to take a harder look at an organization or business. I believe this to be a great tool to analyze self, because it helps us identify factors, both external and internal, that are favorable or unfavorable to achieve a goal. This method can help you discover your strengths, which should be the focus, and areas for improvement, which only provide you with a trait that needs to be conquered.

STRENGTHS

- What advantages do you have that others don't have (e.g., skills, certifications, education, connections)?
- What do you do better than anyone else?
- What personal resources can you access?
- What do other people see as your strengths?
- Which of your achievements are you most proud of?
- What values do you believe in that others fail to exhibit?
- Are you part of a network or a group?

Consider your strengths from your own perspective and from the point of view of the people around you. Don't be modest or shy; be as objective as you can.

WEAKNESSES

- What tasks do you usually avoid because you don't feel comfortable doing them?
- What do the people around you see as your weaknesses?
- In which areas are you weak, in your education and skills training?
- What are your bad work habits? (For example, are you often late, disorganized, short-tempered, or poor at handling stress?)
- Do you have personality traits that hold you back? For instance, are you afraid of speaking in public?

Again, consider this from a personal perspective and an external perspective. Do other people see weaknesses that you don't see? Be realistic—if you don't identify your weaknesses, you won't be able to work on them.

OPPORTUNITIES

- Do you have a network of contacts to help you, or offer good advice?
- What new technology can help you? Or can you get help from others or from people via the Internet?
- Do you have specific skills (like a second language)?

You might find useful opportunities in the following: networking events, educational classes, training, or conferences.

Look at your strengths, and ask yourself whether these open up any opportunities. Then look at your weaknesses, and ask yourself whether you could open up opportunities by eliminating those weaknesses.

THREATS

- What obstacles do you currently face at business, work, home, or school?
- Are any of your co-workers or other businesses competing with you for projects, roles, or status?
- Is your job/business (or the demand for the things you do at home or at school) changing?
- Does changing technology threaten your ability to be successful?
- Could any of your weaknesses lead to threats?

Continue to do this exercise regularly, and reevaluate once or even twice per year. Remember, the analysis helps to determine whether the objective can be attained. If not, then it can be modified to make it attainable. The first aim of the analysis is to assess your strengths, which can be helpful in attaining the objective. The second aim of the analysis is to assess your weaknesses, which can be harmful in attaining the objective. The third aim of the analysis is to assess your opportunities, which include the external conditions that are helpful in attaining the objective. And finally, the fourth aim of the analysis is to assess your threats, which include the external conditions that could impede the attainment of the objective.

Additional Tips to Improve Self-Confidence:

- Don't compare yourself to other people.
- Focus on what you can do, not what you can't do.
- Write down one small goal, each day or each week, that you can accomplish.
- Keep track of your accomplishments in a journal.
- Think positively.

Steeping Away from Your Comfort Zone

"The comfort zone is the great enemy of courage and confidence."
– Brian Tracy

The comfort zone is defined in just that way: a place where you feel familiar and safe. It's a space where your daily activities fit a routine and pattern that decreases risk, anxiety, and stress. But is this a good thing? And are we actually decreasing our overall stress in life, or just hiding it under a cloak of comfort?

Think of the thermostat in your home. Everything feels warm and cozy because you have it set at 70 degrees. You're neither hot nor cold, but just right. We humans are born as creatures of comfort, in love with our neutral state of safety and anticipation—like a child safe in its mother's arms, until they're encouraged to crawl, walk, and talk. So what happens in this zone? Nothing! Or at least nothing new. You sit and are content with the environment around you.

Now don't get me wrong; while in your comfort zone, you may experience consistent and steady results or performance. But if you become too comfortable, you'll start to hold yourself back from tapping into your true greatness. Challenges, and overcoming obstacles, help in your personal growth and development. So are you looking for more? Is average okay, or are you seeking above-average results and optimal performance? If you are, then you'll need to find a method of breaking free from this routine, to embrace stepping away from your comfort zone.

Here are a few methods and benefits on how and why you should step away from your comfort zone.

1. Try New Things (against our native programming, you actually CAN teach an old dog new tricks)

   - Trying new things can enhance creativity. Although creativity will expose you to vulnerability, critics, and possible rejection, you'll more importantly be opening yourself up to great achievement and breakthroughs.
   - Remember Einstein's mindset. Creative people fail, and the really good ones fail often; but those who fail often, will experience greatness!
   - By trying new things, you'll be stepping away from your comfort zone, and the more times you do this, the easier it becomes.
   - Being open to a new experience will enhance your intellect, emotions, imagination, and desire to explore the world around you, and most importantly, the world inside you.

2. Embrace New Challenges

   - Did you know that accepting new challenges can help you age better? A 2013 study, in *Psychology Today*, determined that learning something new, and demanding new life skills, while maintaining a strong social network, can help you stay mentally sharp as you grow older.

3. Say "YES" More Often

    -   Say yes even when you don't think you're ready yet. Take on new assignments at work or in your business.
    -   Accept a new role, especially one that peaks your interest. By saying "YES" more often, you'll break that routine, and may surprise yourself with this new environment.

4. Volunteer

    -   Volunteering can be a great learning experience. By serving others, you'll not only acquire new skills but a profound outlook on the world around you.
    -   At times while you're still figuring out SELF, through your service to others, you'll learn about other perspectives, allowing you to re-examine your own beliefs.
    -   Gratitude! Let's face it; putting yourself in other people's shoes, provides you with a deeper understanding and gratitude for the things you do have in life.

5. PUSH Yourself, But Not Too Far

    -   Get uncomfortable, but never push past optimal anxiety, or performance will drop.

*"My role model didn't tell me;
he (she) showed me."*

— Anonymous

Chapter 6

The Observing YOU
by LAURIEANN

Choose Your Role Models

Choosing your role models is a powerful part of your life.

There are two kinds: the ones you choose to have as your mentors, and the ones you read about and watch, but they are more for your growth in academic learning. Having too many role models as mentors, will confuse you. You need to make sure that you choose one or two maximum as your mentors.

I used to be excited about taking all this training from Brendon Burchard, Anik Singal, Tony Robbins, Mel Robbins, and more. Suddenly, I realized the time it was taking to watch all their training processes. Then I figured out that I had one person who had already submerged himself in all that information, and could coach me and mentor me with his knowledge, which not only encompassed all the big names, but also his amazing brilliance of having worked for 28 years in the area I wanted to exceed in: my market.

Along the way, I met a second person that was in my other desired market. So I am now choosing to be very focused on building my business with these two mentors.

My mentors, Bart Baggett and Raymond Aaron, because I am loyal to them, have also become my friends. What is even more wonderful is that I have had the opportunity to have lunch and dinner with them, one on one. They may not be the Tony Robbins's or the Gary V's of this world, but one is the most famous handwriting expert and forensic expert, who has an amazing background that I admire, and the other is a very smart real estate investor, and more so, on the *New York Times* bestsellers list! His story is inspiring, and both of my mentors are very real, honest, and inspiring.

How did I go about choosing my role models?

There is a secret to success. Take ONE path. Know your path. Find the mentors and the role models that will help you to find that journey and make you successful.

I am not saying to not read about billionaires like Ray Dalio, whom, funnily enough, most people don't know about, and had the insight to what is now happening (my daughter introduced me to him), or the other ones that I noted earlier. It's great to read about their successes. However, when it comes to YOU, pick two of the most important people that will guide YOU through YOUR branding purpose. You know what you want to be, and the "avatars" you want to connect with.

(By the way, I don't like the word AVATAR. It has just become another BUZZ WORD. People are not AVATARS—my preference is "those who are interested in what you do. People who want to learn from you. People who you can create a real relationship with because you have something in common." When I first got on the Internet there where games. In those games, you created your AVATAR. It was a computer-generated version of something you wanted to be that no one saw the real you behind. Real people are not computer-generated. They are humans. And you can hide behind the AVATAR version. But in business and reaching out to someone, you can't reach out to an AVATAR. My handwriting analysis taught me this. The AVATAR will not give you the version of the real person behind that façade.)

Moving along… Once you have that in mind, find the best mentor in YOUR industry. Pick ONE thing to be specifically focused on, and find your two mentors that can be most advantageous in helping and mentoring you.

It is so important to build a personal "relationship" with your mentors. They will guide you, be honest, be there, and will make sure that all that you need is held in their knowledge and education.

Choose the first one that is the most important; then have a backup with number TWO. But always remember to be loyal to both. You will make a stronger relationship. Also, make sure the two you choose each have their strengths and are not competing for your attention.

For example, I am a handwriting analyst. I want to perfect that, and my marketing skills with that. I chose Bart Baggett to help me with this.

I am also an author. Bart did start into the business of helping new authors, but when he decided this was not his favorite area, I found Raymond Aaron, who helps with that part of my life.

I now have TWO TOP mentors. No more than that. They are who I like to invest in for my journey toward success. By being loyal, I have also built a personal relationship with them that is priceless.

What do you want to excel in? Who would be your NUMBER ONE to be your mentor? Do you know someone willing to give you their time and energy personally, and not pass you over to someone else?

Take inventory. Write down two mentors that you know will be there for you. Then on the other side, write the ones you want to keep learning from. But remember, if you want the attention you require, only pick one or TWO maximum for your life coach/mentors. Trust me; this is valuable advice.

ATTAINABLE PERSONAL   LEARNING FROM MENTORS
MENTORS

_____   _____

_____   _____

_____   _____

_____   _____

_____   _____

To my previous chapter, you want one or two important mentors in your life. Your loyalty to them will reap you amazing rewards.

But I also said not to stop reading about other very successful people. There is a lot to be learned from their books and their life experiences that led them to success. Most successful people have read many libraries full of books by the rich and the famous.

But in my experience, for the last 12 years, it has been truly amazing watching one person grow, and build and fascinate me with the skills that have been developed. Beyond that, there has been humility and strength in building a valuable, smaller, yet strong community.

What I am saying here? It is all that. Read, watch, pay attention. Sometimes the most brilliant minds don't equate to your life achievements. Being realistic is very important. You may find a mentor that is successful in balancing life, and having a great lifestyle, but is not a multi-millionaire. And sometimes they are the ones that teach us the most and are more connected to us on a one-on-one basis. Don't discredit them just because of the lack of zeros at the end of their dollar value. Their zeros may only be five, but that in itself, these days, is a great place to be. I am realistic. My first half a million a year will be so great to look at in my bank account! If they are making six zeros, and the first number is a "1," that too is something to aspire to. I hope you are understanding my point here.

As I stated in my previous chapters, I have been up and down and up and down—I risked, I lost, I risked again, lost again. I tried to be more, too quickly. I tried to achieve too much too fast. I was impatient. I wanted success now.

I have to read several books in my life, but not being an avid "book" reader is not a negative quality. I have spent a lot of years reading articles as well. I tend to find that if I don't have the time to complete a book, my education comes from articles, and I read a lot of those. It is another way of keeping up to date with what is new, what is transpiring, and what you need to know in the now.

Again, read, watch, and pay attention. Learn, grow, and be patient. Very few ever become a millionaire overnight, so don't knock yourself down for not being one. Very few become a glowing success overnight. YOUR brand will take time. And YOUR brand alone will not make you successful. Your hard work and moving forward with YOUR brand to build relationships, will make you a success.

My father always reminded me that I was a turtle. But he also reminded me that in the tale of "The Turtle and the Hare," the turtle won. I will take that as a compliment. And it complements my life now. I tried to be "the hare," and forgot I was "the turtle." With this in mind, I now know I have to be consistent. I have to walk forward with a plan, determination, and knowing that the finish line is there, but I don't have to run toward it; I just have to keep sight of it.

Another point: You can also spend too much time reading, watching, and paying attention. You then lose the race. When you finally know what you want to do, and have done enough research, reading, watching, and paying attention, put your side blinders on and get going. It's a known fact that a runner will lose seconds off their time if they look sideways to see where their competition is. Look forward. Pay attention, but keep your side blinders on as well. You will be amazed at the results and the success you will achieve when you stop trying to compete against them, and start doing the best YOU can do for yourself.

Test: How much time do you spend on reading, watching, and paying attention to others, versus doing your part with forward steps for your business?

Balance. At some point, you just have TO DO.

Imitate, Mimic, Practice

To imitate, mimic, and practice what others are doing, may take away from the TRUE YOU.

Do you believe that sentence to be true?

It's not.

Pay attention, make notes of what you like about someone successful, and integrate it. This is not losing YOU; this is making you a better person, and likely more confident.

Ever since I was 3, I wanted to be an actress. It was my dream, but my parents laughed. I'm not sure if this desire was from watching my dad up on stage singing in an operetta, or from watching the movies of Shirley Temple. Or it may have just been in my soul. I know that many children feel that way, but this was real. This was more than just a whimsical thought.

I like the limelight, but I am also an introvert at the same time. I like my time alone. Interesting duality. And I will admit that it confused me when I was younger, because how can you be an actor, or a speaker, or someone famous, if you are also driven to hide?

However, as I watched actors and famous people, I realized that a lot of them are like me. What makes them interesting and intriguing is that they are like chameleons. They shine when they are out there, and then they disappear into their much desired, secret, hidden world.

I learned to imitate it at a young age. If there was a trait in someone I liked, I would take it as my own, and implement it into my character on a day-to-day basis. Some say that reading and learning helps you the most, but I believe learning to build your character by being able to recognize traits you admire in others, and uniting it with your individualism, is a gift. This is the gift of imitation and mimicking, and this integration happens with practice.

How does this serve you?

This serves you by being perceptive enough to find those qualities that others admire, and being able to add them to your strengths. It's not being fake, as some might think here; it is being smart. If you can take on a character of someone else, and it feels perfectly normal for you, then it is a part of you that you just didn't see in yourself, but you did in another. Is it stealing someone's character to become someone you are not? No. It's integrating someone's character that you admire, to make yourself better, and that likely you always possessed but just didn't know it. It's part of your chameleon.

Now, with all this said, you have to choose the color of YOUR brand. Are you orange? Blue? Green? Red? (Colors are associated with character.) When you are out there and building your public image, pick a color. You can be any color you want when you leave that "image" and go home to your family. But when you are out there, be that color you choose. Imitate it, mimic it, and never stop practicing it. Because that IS a big part of YOU out there, and YOUR brand.

Most of you out there are a chameleon as I am, but make sure you are that same color when you are out in public.

Let's have fun. Pick 5 traits of your favorite person, who is either famous in your industry, an actor, or even a friend. What color would you associate them with?

PERSON   **COLOR**

_____   _____

_____   _____

_____   _____

_____   _____

_____   _____

_____   _____

Scribble, Doodle, Map

This is my favorite thing to do. I scribble on paper, and doodle and draw maps of where I want to go. Quite often, I end up with all sorts of little papers here and there, with these on them.

Recently, I have learned to either paste them or staple them into a diary or journal, and date them. This will be the shortest chapter, but the most fun.

Take three things you want to scribble about, like a child would; then doodle your thoughts after the scribble, and lay out a map of where you want to be in 5 years. Here is mine. Have fun creating yours.

Observe YOU

Observing yourself is very tough. It may be intimidating when you hear something from someone else about your behavior, or your posture, or your clothes. But the truth is, it's even worse when you observe YOU.

I remember doing my first "lives" on Facebook. I wasn't as horrified as I thought I would be, but I could see every little part of my flaws.

That is what most of us do. It's not just other people's comments; it's quite often your thoughts about yourself that are the biggest roadblock to moving forward and succeeding.

I had fun doing a 30-day challenge for myself, and posting every day. Ummm, ah, amazing: These were my repetitions, and they still are. It would be wise for me to take some courses in public speaking to further my knowledge of how to eliminate those. But here is the thing. People watched anyway, and they liked it, because when I was doing my "lives," I was just ME.

Can I improve? Absolutely, but it takes time. And surprisingly, I started liking myself better. It wasn't because I was a great speaker; it was because I stood up to my challenge, and I completed it.

When you are observing YOU, don't just look at your presentation. You need to observe your determination, your courage, and your positive traits, such as helping others. NO ONE IS PERFECT.

What is even more fun is falling in love with your imperfections. Quite often, your audience will relate more to those than your perfections. Those allow them to feel a bond, a relationship with you, even if they don't know you.

So when observing YOU, yes, you should understand that there are certain areas that you can always improve on, but to stop yourself from doing something because, when you are observing YOU, you are focusing on the negatives, it won't work. Make a list of the positives. Focus on those, and take courses to ameliorate those areas you perhaps feel could use some help —like eliminating the "ummm, ah, amazing" repetitions. ☺

I challenge you to do five Facebook lives or recorded ZOOMs, and then write down five positives, and five areas you feel you can improve on.

POSITIVES   **NEED FOR IMPROVEMENT**

_____   _____

_____   _____

_____   _____

_____   _____

_____   _____

"Risks must be taken because the greatest hazard in life is to risk nothing."
– **Leo F. Buscaglia,**
Living, Loving and Learning

The Comfort Zone *(by Being You)*

Hopefully, the exercise above helped you to become more comfortable in your skin. If it didn't, then repeat it. 😊

I found this interesting chart. There are two versions of being in the comfort zone. One is being too comfortable in your life situation; the other one is being comfortable being YOU. These are two different versions. Don't confuse them.

Being comfortable in your life situation zone will not help you to find success. It may create a negative effect on your life. If you are not a risk taker, you will remain in that secure zone and not likely achieve what you aspire to, if you are aspiring to succeed.

Years ago, when I was in my 20s, I fell in love with the books by Leo Buscaglia, after a friend of mine gave one to me, with a very powerful quote he guided me to. After reading that first book, I read all Leo Buscaglia's books. I also wrote to him often, and he always wrote me back. (I still have all his letters). I even invited him to my wedding, and he responded that he would have loved to be there but had a previous engagement. True? I don't know, but I still have the letter. 😊

A few years later, I met him when I lived in Reno. It was such an honor. I still have a signed copy of one of his books, from that day.

But I digress. The point is, this man wrote about love. Not just love of a man and a woman or a couple, but also of a love of self. It is important to not just love others, but more so to love yourself enough to take chances in relationships and life—to love life enough to take a chance on living!

Leo gave me permission to use one of his quotes in a book I wrote back in my 20s (never published, but I still have the manuscript), and it was this, the quote my friend had highlighted:

"The person who risks nothing does nothing, has nothing, is nothing, and becomes nothing. He may avoid suffering and sorrow, but he simply cannot learn, feel, change, grow, or love. Chained by his certitude, he is a slave; he has forfeited his freedom. Only the person who risks is truly free."

– Leo Buscaglia

POWERFUL. It has guided my life ever since. It's been my destiny, for better or for worse.

Live in the comfort of YOU knowing you have done what you dreamed about—not in the comfort zone of what you have not.

"The Comfort Zone"

| Comfort Zone | Fear Zone | Learning Zone | Growth Zone |

Lack self-confidence

Deal with challenges and problems

Find purpose

Live dreams

Feel safe and in control

Find excuses

Acquire new skills

Set new goals

Be affected by others' opinions

Extend your comfort zone

Conquer objectives

"When you journal your life, or document your daily activities in writing, you're not only recording and expressing yourself; YOU are CREATING yourself!"
– **Robert Max Wall**

CHAPTER 7

Maintaining the Motivated YOU
by Robert Max Wall

Preparing for More and Stepping into Your Own

So, now that you're discovering more about YOU, possibly more than you ever expected, how does one stay motivated?

Here are a few proven methods to staying on course. This won't happen all at once, but by focusing on those elements of branding YOU—health, happiness, passion, purpose, and being appreciative and in tune with YOU—you'll experience breakthroughs, and advance to a higher version of yourself.

1. Build a business around your passion.

   When you do something you truly love, it's not hard to find the motivation required to succeed. If you are involved in an industry that bores you, it will be difficult to dig down deep and capture that motivation when you need it. You have to be truly passionate about what you are doing.

   I started my coaching/consulting career in 1993, after several other business ventures, because after weighing out both my successes and failed attempts, I recognized that it was the people (peers, employees, contractors, mentors, clients, community) that I was truly passionate about. My purpose to see others advance and obtain their dreams, is the catalyst for my own motivation. I wake up motivated every morning, simply because I love what I do.

But passions can change, and it's important that you evolve with them. For example, from the time I could spell "business," I knew I wanted one. I was fortunate to have mentors in my life at a very young age, and inherently knew deep within my core that I would be a business owner. But prior to going all-in on helping others find their true passions, conquer their fears, and dominate their markets, I owned other businesses. In fact, business after business, because I knew I was passionate about being an entrepreneur and a business owner; but I had not yet found my true purpose or whom I wanted to serve. A 24-year leap forward, I know without a doubt what my purpose is, and whom I want to serve; and soon enough, you'll find yours too. Continue to follow your passion, and you will seldom lack motivation.

"Every great dream begins with a dreamer. Always remember, you have within you the strength, the patience, and the passion to reach for the stars to change the world."
– Harriet Tubman

2. Always have both long and short-term goals.

I'm a big advocate of setting goals. Long-term goals give you something to work toward, and by including short-term goals, you're ensuring that you are able to seize victory consistently, providing further motivation to push hard toward achieving those long-term goals and visions.

Every single person is unique, and may prove multiple ways of staying on track; but over the years, I've witnessed a trend with highly successful people: Their goals are written down, and they have them accessible and review them daily. Whether in their face, like a whiteboard in their office, or on their phone with reminder alerts, or in that trusty notebook, successful individuals visualize goals, record them, and take action on them.

With me personally, I function better with both the whiteboard and notebook method. This constant visualization helps me stay motivated and 100-percent focused on setting my defined goals, reviewing them daily, and monitoring my progress, resulting in regular motivation.

"If you want to be happy, set a goal that commands your thoughts, liberates your energy, and inspires your hopes."
– Andrew Carnegie

3. Be extremely optimistic.

When you are consistently optimistic, you focus on just the positives, which helps you stay motivated and focused on reaching your goals. The minute you start to bring negative thoughts into play, is the same moment your forward momentum will come to an abrupt halt.

Does the possibility of failure exist? Absolutely, but you can't think this way. Entrepreneurs, visionaries, and leaders need to think like Olympic athletes. Do you think that for one moment a gold medal Olympian focused their mindset on losing every race? I'm willing to bet that the possibility of losing was still present, but they never allowed this to enter their mind. Their optimism dominated their thoughts, blocking out all negativity, and only focusing on the goal at hand.

4. Commit to the end goal.

Success often comes to those who take big risks, and big risks can result in epic failures. There are very few one-hit wonders, as most successful entrepreneurs have experienced failure at one point.

Even if you have failed in the past, commit to your end goal, and don't think about those past failures or the possibility of failing again. Could it happen? Yes, but you could also be the next great success story. This circles back to the point above: You must remain extremely optimistic at all times, and if you get knocked down, you have to bounce right back up, 100-percent focused on your end goal.

5. Surround yourself with like-minded people.

   This is probably the most important element, so I'll say it again but louder... SURROUND YOURSELF WITH LIKE-MINDED PEOPLE! It has been proven that the company you surround yourself with has a direct influence on how you behave, both in your personal life and in the workplace. This quote by Michael Dell fits perfectly:

"Try never to be the smartest person in the room. And if you are, I suggest you invite smarter people ... or find a different room. In professional circles, it's called networking. In organizations, it's called team building. And in life, it's called family, friends, and community. We are all gifts to each other, and my own growth as a leader has shown me again and again that the most rewarding experiences come from my relationships."
– Michael Dell

Design Your Rituals Around Essential Habits of Organization in Life and Business

Even if someone you know or observe appears to be extremely organized, they were not born this way. They had to cultivate healthy habits, which in turn helped them to stay organized.

So even if you think you are a very disorganized person, you can learn effective habits to becoming organized. From planning things, jotting things down, to ditching the unnecessary, and organizing things that matter, you will become an organized person as long as you're willing to learn and practice.

Here are a few essential habits on how to become organized, and in maintaining organization:

1. Write Things Down

    We all know someone that remembers every birthday and sends cards for every holiday. It's not magic, and they don't use memorization. Trying to remember things will not help you to stay organized. You should try writing things down.

    A pen and some paper is our way of remembering things externally, and it's much more permanent.

    You will only further complicate your life by trying to contain important dates and reminders in your head. Write down everything: shopping lists for groceries, holiday gifts, home decor, and important dates like meetings and birthdays.

    As an experiment, try writing down people's names shortly after you meet them (when they're not looking). I'll bet you remember a lot more names that way.

2. Make Schedules and Deadlines

    Organized people don't waste time. They recognize that keeping things organized goes hand in hand with staying productive. They make and keep schedules for the day and week. They make deadlines and set goals. And most importantly, they stick to them!

    Similarly, by living a cluttered lifestyle, you will not have the time or space to make your deadlines or achieve your goals. As an experiment, look at your bucket list, or make one. Write down the things you want to achieve this year or in your life. Then write down what you need to do to achieve them. Life is too short, so make sure you're doing what matters most in life.

3. Avoid Procrastinating

The longer you wait to do something, the more difficult it will be to get it done. Is it okay for me to admit that when LaurieAnn asked me to co-author this book, I enthusiastically leaped at the offer (thank you LA), but fell into procrastination with so many other tasks at hand. How do you eat an elephant? One bite at a time. If you want your life to be less stressful and less demanding, then organize as soon as you can, and prioritize effectively. Putting in the effort to get things done as soon as possible will lift the weight off of you from doing it later, resulting in more productivity and a happy, healthy life.

As an experiment, think of one thing that you should organize in your life. Write it down. Then write down when you can accomplish it and what you'll require to meet that task. If you can get it done right now, then just go do it!

4. Give Everything a Home

It's easy to get lost if you don't have a home. Keeping your life organized means keeping your things in their own designated places. Organized people keep order by storing things properly and by labeling storage spaces.

Make easy-to-access storage spaces for things you use all the time, and prevent your storage spaces from getting cluttered. Be creative about finding places for things. In addition, as a BIG NO: Never label a storage space or a file as "miscellaneous!"

As an experiment, choose one place in your home, work, or office, that you can re-organize. If there are scattered items, then group them together. Once you've sorted everything, find or make a "home" for similar items, label the "homes," and put the items in the proper spaces.

5. Declutter Regularly

    Find time each week to organize. Highly organized people make sure they find time, every week or more, to organize their things. Stuff does not stay organized on its own; it needs to be reorganized continuously and consistently.

    Add this task to your schedule: clerical time, office time, rotation of files, bills, etc. It's only going to get done if you schedule the time and execute the task.

6. Keep Only What You Need

    More stuff means more clutter. People who live organized lives only keep what they need and what they really, really want. Having fewer things also means that you enjoy those things more, and feel better about using everything you own, rather than letting half of what you own collect dust.

    Have you ever felt like you don't have the space to keep all the stuff you own? Instead of renting a storage unit or buying a larger home, get rid of some things.

    As an experiment, write down the number of things you think you actually need. Then write a list of all the things that you own. If the number of things you actually own exceeds your ideal need list, then it's time to organize.

7. Know Where to Discard Items

    Do whatever you can to get rid of stuff. Less stuff means less clutter. Here are some ideas:

- Donate to thrift stores
- Sell on Craigslist, Marketplace, or eBay
- Take a trip to the recycling center
- Set up a garage sale
- Find a shelter or local charity to get rid of your things. Remember, FREE goes quicker!

Exercise: Choose one space in your house or office to completely purge. Go through everything. Anything you find that you don't use regularly, sort for review later. If it's NOT needed at all, SCRAP it immediately!

8. Delegate Responsibilities

A really organized life is not overfilled with responsibilities, meetings, and deadlines. In fact, it has less, because things that create stress have been slowly organized out.

As an experiment, look at your to-do list, or make one. Go through the list and find one task that you can remove from your list or give to someone else. Now feel the stress of having to do it fall away.

9. Work Hard

Put in a little effort. Actually, put in a lot of effort when necessary.

Once you have delegated responsibilities and made a schedule, then you can organize the task, and then prioritize based on what needs to be done and when you are able do it.

Staying organized is not all a breeze. It requires that you work hard with recognition that when you work harder, you can enjoy your clutter-free home, life, and office later.

Work harder when you feel like giving up today.

"Inaction breeds doubt and fear. Action breeds confidence and courage. If you want to conquer fear, do not sit home and think about it. Go out and get busy."
– Dale Carnegie

Document Your Progress Toward Success

"Our goals can only be reached through a vehicle of plan, in which we must fervently believe, and upon which we must vigorously act. There is no other route to success."
– Pablo Picasso

As human beings, we're hardwired to want to reach the finish line. We crave completion, crossing items off a to-do list and saying we're finished, so that we can move on to the next big thing.

However, all of this obsession with saying we're "done," can lead to what's called completion bias, where your brain specifically seeks the hit of dopamine you get from crossing off small tasks, and ignores working on larger, more complex ones.

But not everything is so easily measured. Large (and often more meaningful) projects don't get crossed off in a single day.

To stay committed to the work that matters most, we need to find ways to measure, track, and feel good about the progress we make daily.

Always remember that small wins are major motivators and should be executed regularly to gain momentum; however, the small ones that are hard to measure are at many times ignored.

So why are both small and even some large advances lost throughout the day? We overlook them and fail to notice them, because we lack a method for tracking this progress. What's even worse is that it is only we that can make this change within our environment.

Most corporate settings leave people feeling depressed and defeated. Here are just a few reasons this happens: The day is filled with meaningless busy work; many companies have lost the ability to set effective goals; there's no real way to track this progress, and if there is, most systems used for employee review are worthless in detail, depth of the character, regular communication, or integration into the companies' true objectives.

Here are 5 ways to stop being just busy, and to start tracking effectively:

1. Dissect large tasks into smaller ones, and then map them out to better visualize them. Break the big goals into smaller ones, then the smaller ones into your daily, weekly, and monthly tasks.

2. Set every day at ZERO.

   Edith Harbaugh, CEO of LaunchDarkly, uses the following technique: *"Once your direction is set, begin each day with a blank slate. Starting every day from zero increases team focus, generates a concrete sense of accomplishment and forward motion, and helps prevent complacency."*

3. Utilize an automated approach to track specific goals. Whether it's just an alarm set on your calendar/phone, or something more comprehensive, like RescueTime, Time Doctor, Toggl or Staff, using a method for task tracking and daily activity, helps tremendously and boosts productivity in no time!

4. Use your existing calendar system to track metrics. As basic as this is, it will allow you to look back at a couple of regular tasks to gage progress. A perfect example of this would be daily sales calls, compared to closed sales.

5. Journal! Journaling is one of the best practices you can have in improving yourself, your brand, and your business. Journal for 10 minutes minimum per day. Include your wins, temporary setbacks, and any resources required to improve upon your success.

> *"People who keep journals have life twice."*
> – Jessamyn West

Chapter 8

YOU Need Social Media Omni-Presence
by LAURIEANN

YOU Are at the Front *(Once Your Business Is Created, You Have to Stand in Front of Your Product)*

Now, how do you do that? Find the perfect person who can help you build your success.

Pardon, you may say? Yes. It is worth the investment to connect with people with influence. However, don't be fooled. Make sure that person who is offering you a great opportunity is available to you. Make sure it is someone who recognizes your abilities.

I have spoken to my mentors, Bart Baggett and Raymond Aaron, and just added a new one— Forbes Riley—as this book was being written.

She taught me how to believe in how to present my perfect pitch in a different way: ENTHUSIASM for what you are offering as a service or product. If you are LIVE, you have to show them how excited you are about the service or product. And you need to be genuine.

The strange thing is, I always do much better if I can say, "I LOVE THIS, and I KNOW you will too!!" Passion, presence—share your passion... your presence.

And make sure you have the SIGNATURE that shows SUCCESS! The *signature* is not just YOUR SIGNATURE, which means a lot, but it is also YOUR CHARACTER signature that they hear in your voice, with your honesty and integrity.

L.I.F.T.

What is **LIFT**? LinkedIn, Instagram, Facebook and Twitter. I am LaurieAnn, and I love the word "LIFT."   One night, I realized that it actually was also perfect as an acronym for social media, and I decided to own it, but I am now sharing it with you to easily remember your most important audiences.

Wordpress and Jetpack are testimonials to the top 4.

LinkedIn, **I**nstagram, **F**acebook and **T**witter: **LIFT**

This is not telling you that you should actually send everything at the same time, but it helps. Note: Depending on your industry, we will need to advise you that posting to get your target market is clearly defined on the time and day you post.

I do realize there is Snapchat, TikTok, and many others, but these (LIFT) have been the mainstay for quite some time.

You can LIFT with Jetpack with just one Wordpress blog. It's quick and delivered immediately.

I am not advocating that Jetpack is the only solution; I'm sharing with you the ease of multiple posts with just one click of the "publish" button.

This is a very short chapter, because this is the message:

To build your presence, LIFT yourself.

"L.I.F.T. YOUR BRAND."

Go LIVE, as Often as YOU Can!!

And this is NOT about being VAIN or having an EGO. (By the way, positive EGOS are not bad at all.)

Get out there! Tell people how passionate you are, and don't worry if you are NOT PERFECT.

Fun thought: Don't you just love people who are genuine, and tell you on a LIVE that they are spooked? I love those who take the risk of someone saying, "Really? You are saying *ummmm* too much," or "Nice presentation, but stop saying, *ahhhhh*."

My fun thought: Those people that speak to them about their mistakes? GREAT! Because you don't learn without criticism. (May I say, though, that delivery to the person making the effort should be kind.)

In time, LIVES will become your friend. Why? Because people watching you, for the most part, will just enjoy the fact that you had the ability to do that, and are sharing something that matters to them.

NEVER QUIT.

CHAPTER 9

It's Time for YOU to LEVEL UP!
by Robert Max Wall

Ready, Mindset, GO!

Mindset is EVERYTHING! Mindset is probably the most critical component in every aspect of life, as it takes the thoughts of your mind to control your actions.

A strong, growth mindset helps us to overcome obstacles and seize opportunities, while a weak, fixed mindset can trap us in a self-defeating cycle.

"If you change the way you look at things,
the things you look at change."
– Wayne Dyer

"Life has no limitations except the ones you make."
– Les Brown

To better understand mindset, here are the definitions of both a growth and a fixed mindset.

A "fixed mindset" assumes that our characters, intelligence, and creative abilities are static absolutes that we cannot change in any meaningful way, and that success is the affirmation of that inherent intelligence, an assessment of how those absolutes measure up against an equally fixed standard; striving for success and avoiding failure at all costs becomes a way of maintaining the sense of being smart or skilled.

A "growth mindset," on the other hand, thrives on challenge and sees failure not as evidence of unintelligence but as a heartening springboard for growth and for stretching our existing abilities. Out of these two mindsets, which we manifest from a very early age, springs a great deal of our behavior, our relationship with success and failure in both professional and personal contexts, and ultimately, our capacity for happiness.

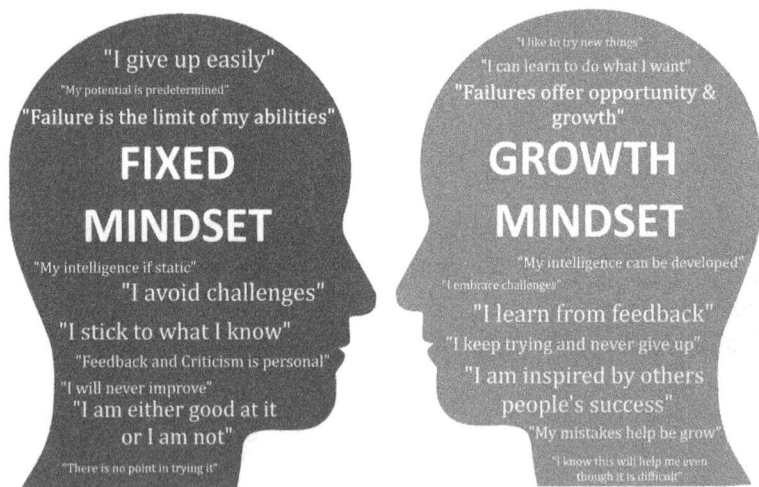

FIXED MINDSET

"I give up easily"
"My potential is predetermined"
"Failure is the limit of my abilities"
"My intelligence if static"
"I avoid challenges"
"I stick to what I know"
"Feedback and Criticism is personal"
"I will never improve"
"I am either good at it or I am not"
"There is no point in trying it"

GROWTH MINDSET

"I like to try new things"
"I can learn to do what I want"
"Failures offer opportunity & growth"
"My intelligence can be developed"
"I embrace challenges"
"I learn from feedback"
"I keep trying and never give up"
"I am inspired by others people's success"
"My mistakes help be grow"
"I know this will help me even though it is difficult"

By now, if you are truly being honest with yourself… Which mindset are you functioning in today? How has this mindset affected your life, both positively and negatively? Regardless of your answer, the good news is that you can take back control of your mind today. And if you can control your mind, YOU GAIN CONTROL of your life!

Make a list of what your life would look like tomorrow if you were instantly able to gain full control.

1. Faith?
2. Relationship with spouse or partner?
3. Children or other family members?
4. Environment – Where you work and live?
5. Finances?
6. Your service or contribution to help others?

For a further, in-depth study on mindset and how you can reprogram your life, LaurieAnn and I would like to invite you as our guest, to our next upcoming boot camp, "Ready, Mindset, Go!"

Heartset – The New Oxygen

Everyone wants to focus on mindset, which is one of the most crucial ingredients to branding YOU, and toward achieving success overall. But what's the driving force behind your desire to improve self?

Heartset is a deep desire to improve and achieve all things in life. It's the true catalyst behind your WHY. Fulfilling your heart's desire is almost a necessity for your soul—almost as important as water to drink and air to breathe!

By opening up your heart to all situations, possibilities, and environments, not only does it provide you with the catalyst to make a change or to help others, it also protects and prevents you from becoming disconnected from the world and the things most important in life. Heartset maintains your humanity above your deep desire to achieve success.

By complementing your strong mindset with heartset, you'll be destined to provide value to not only yourself but to others around you. Your clients, employees, subordinates, peers, friends, and family will all benefit from your heartset. Heartset will bring value and inspiration to the multitude.

How to develop and expand your heartset:

1. Ask yourself who you want to serve in life. What matters most to you (e.g., faith, family, friends)?
2. Question your feelings. Does this empower you?
3. STOP taking everything personally. Does LIFE happen for or against you? Your response matters.
4. Relationships over transactions; value over taking.

Mastermind Your Manners – Master Self, Before Others

Now that your personal brand and your purpose has been discovered and developed, and is on its way to perfection, what's next?

We have talked a great deal about discovering self and staying closely connected around the campfire, with those who are like-minded, and those who will lift you up, challenge you, and celebrate the NEW YOU! Another great way of maintaining this transformation, and protecting the time, emotion, energy, and even the investment you've poured into SELF, is through a mastermind.

A mastermind is taking a step beyond the campfire. It's a place where others, like yourself, are ready to not just talk but truly take things to the next level. Each mastermind offers something uniquely different, but all have the same goal in mind: achieve success, grow in wisdom and purpose, and always pay these rewards forward.

Mastermind groups are still a relatively new concept to most people and organizations, even though Napoleon Hill created the concept over 80 years ago, with his book, *Think and Grow Rich* (recommended top-10 reader).

In a mastermind, members of the group will challenge each other in discovery, goal setting, and staying on course through accountability. Accountability is KEY. Many capable, future visionaries and leaders of today, lose their motivation and desire with the absence of accountability.

Here are a few reasons to join a mastermind, and how to get started right away:

1. Extend your current network or tribe: In a mastermind, not only do you and your tribe grow through this higher level of thinking, but your network will expand by this increased exposure to the group, and by being around their tribes as well.
2. Advisement and mentoring: You're no longer alone. You now have access to other advisors, and can contribute your expertise to others as well.
3. Exclusive VIP status: Many times, these mastermind groups offer access to information and additional levels of training that even an elite education system can't offer. Some memberships are so

exclusive that they even carry their own notoriety and credibility in the world of business.

4. Collaboration is essential in achieving your goals in both life and business: By joining a mastermind, you may align yourself with another member that helps fill a gap on one of your projects. Or they may need your expertise and contribution as well. More is achieved together.

To get started, see our list of masterminds at every level.

Your Modern Day Resumé

So now that you're discovering more about YOU, possibly more than you ever expected, and you now have some new tools on how to stay motivated and connected, how do you deliver your message to the masses?

The day of the "traditional resume" is slowly fading away. To understand the impact of delivering YOU the right way, place yourself in the hiring manager's or interviewer's shoes. A stack of traditional resumes, or a list of people to interview for a bid, speaking engagement, or live show, are unfortunately a dime a dozen. Most people seeking talent or the next best story, are overworked, at times underpaid, and almost always short on time. If you want to woo these individuals, you must offer more than what the other 100 resumes or biographies, sitting in front of them, are offering.

YOU can achieve all of this and so much more, by differentiating yourself from the norm. These 4 elements are considered to be your keys to personal branding, advertising, marketing, sales, building your audience, your resume, and even a replacement of that traditional business card!

1. Your Story

I talk a great deal about storytelling in my soon-to-be-released book, *YOU Are the Product.* Resumes don't always tell the whole story, results, accolades, acknowledgments, or transformational experience. But your story, carefully crafted into your bio, will set you apart from those 100 other common templates found online.

People buy from those they know, like, and trust! I can't emphasize this enough. And if a complete stranger has anywhere from 60 seconds to 30 minutes to get to know you, you must deliver the content of your life through story.

There's a story for every occasion, and you'll need to know how to research, prepare, and deliver each of them, when the time is best suited.

From time to time, we host a storytelling session online. Visit www.makeupnotrequired.com for upcoming webinars.

2. Podcasts or Vidcasts

A podcast, both audio only and video, is a great way to deliver your message. In fact, when compared to email or a mailed letter, it's statistically proven that this format will not only reach a greater number of people in your audience, but they'll be more perceptive when they hear your voice or see your expressions.

One of the reasons that podcasts are so engaging, and foster such loyal audiences, is because they are very interactive. Hosts can create audience polls, answer questions, and take "calls," just like a traditional radio show.

Because podcasts are delivered digitally, they eliminate many costs associated with other forms of communication, including postage, printing, and paper. They can also reduce meeting costs and e-mail storage costs. They are easy to archive, and updating them is quick and easy.

3. **Speaking Live from Stage and on Radio!**

Feeling sick when you go on stage? Great suggestion: Do you know that "fear" and "excitement" are intertwined? So when you need to get on a show, live on Facebook, stage, or radio, just think of that "fear" as EXCITEMENT, and butterflies in the stomach as being the best feeling ever, like when you were a child. Guess what? That IS what you are feeling. Not fear, but excitement. And when you understand that, it becomes easier to face "the crowds."

Not EVERYONE is going to LOVE you. But as long as you are enthusiastic and passionate about what you're delivering, it doesn't matter. You don't want the negative people there anyway, and most people who "hate" are just not happy with themselves. As long as you are, don't worry. Keep going.

4. Writing Your Book

Wow. We just did this. We wrote our book. And you can collaborate with a book. Do you know how much it means to engage someone with even just ONE page in your book, and that you can acknowledge them? It SPEAKS VOLUMES to COLLABORATION. It doesn't take much. LaurieAnn and I wrote most of this book. But we have a great team in the Advanced Branding Collaborative, so each will have one page to share their thoughts about collaboration. THAT IS collaboration.

Mastermind *(connect with other like-minded entrepreneurs – groups, etc.)*

It is worth the investment. But make sure you are investing in a mastermind that is going to not only connect you, but even more so, build relationships that are interactive. What I find even more important is the friendship you build with the mastermind behind the mastermind. ☺

My personal experience is that you can follow some masterminds where the person is too busy to give you a one-on-one. I get it. They are too big to spread themselves thin with their millions of followers. I really enjoy learning from these mastermind people on one front, but my favorite masterminds, behind the mastermind groups, are the ones that are successful but still have the time to reach out to me, to become a lifelong friend over the years of loyalty and connection. Even if they are not a Tony Robbins or a Gary V or a Brendon Burchard, they are achieving something you want to achieve—6 figures.

Do you know my mentors or mastermind behind my mastermind groups? Maybe, maybe not. I will say that my knowledge has come from them, and I thank them for the times that I text them and get almost an immediate response. That is a gift, and one that you will not get from the top 10. But you will get it from someone equally as successful in my world. These are people who are truly serving without serving themselves. They are truly there for you when you need them—priceless.

Chapter 10

Congrats YOU! Elations! YOU Are the Brand! by LAURIEANN

YOU Are the Brand! What's Next?

Make sure your pictures remain the same. People will relate to you better if you stay consistent. And with this, ENJOY the journey!

Make sure your SIGNATURE speaks to YOU.

Make sure your PICTURE speaks to YOU.

Make sure your PASSION speaks to YOU.

Make sure you KEEP sending that message.

And finally,

MAKE SURE YOU ARE TRUE TO YOU.

Fans Versus Followers

I prefer FANS to FOLLOWERS.

However, **I prefer loyal people** in relation to the above statement. Here is why..

You can have both: fans and followers. But the true value, in business and creating your brand, is in *who you have really created a relationship with.*

This takes MORE time than just having FANS and FOLLOWERS.

You need to find time to respond. To reach out. To become someone that they feel can be "touched," metaphorically speaking.

If someone reaches out to you, and you don't respond, you are sending the message that you are TOO BUSY and that they are not worth your time to even just say, "I am busy, but please contact me at such a time". It belittles your brand and YOU if you don't have the compassion, empathy, sympathy, or humanity to take ONE SMALL MOMENT to respond. Your clients or customers, and even your family and friends remember this. It also takes 2 seconds to say "please" or "thank you".

Instead of a FAN or a FOLLOWER, I would prefer to think of the person as someone who just wants me to reach out and say, "I AM HERE."

I know this takes time, and it's sometimes exhausting, but it is worth it.

Sharing the Brand New YOU

SMILE!! BE ENTHUSIASTIC.. and share that!!
This chapter doesn't need to say much more than that.
And share, as mentioned before, as **a L.I.F.T.!!!**

- LinkedIn
- Instagram
- Facebook
- Twitter

There are more, but it's nice to keep it to just four. So the above may not be your choices... but find 4. And keep to it.

SHARE!

This brings us back to Jetpack. Or even WordPress with share buttons. One place allows you to SHARE, in 2 minutes, to many.

Contact us at www.makeupnotrequired.com for more information on how to share everywhere, in literally less than 5 minutes.

Make GREAT Choices; After All, You Have a Brand to Protect

I think you all know this about making great choices. Just don't post things you might be sorry for later.

Make sure that someone isn't out there stealing your ideas. Check if someone copied your website, and used a different ending. (e.g., .com versus .net)

And watch your #tags. Some people use yours, and it is a bit disturbing what they post.

Be SMART: Sensible, Marketable, Aware, Ready, and Tantalizing.

Manifest Your Destiny *(There Are No Ceilings; the Only Limitations Are the Ones You Place on Yourself)*

How do you best do this?

VISION BOARD!!

I remember doing a vision board in 2010. I have to admit, it was pathetic. What I hoped for was minimal.

I realized that MANIFESTING is about thinking BIG!!

Here is my story on this.

I wanted to marry the man I met at a birthday party, when I was 18. I looked at him and went back to my friends and said, "I just met my future husband." Seven years later, I married him.

Was it perfect? At the beginning, yes. But things got complicated, and after 22 years of loving him, we divorced. I still love him. I still love the man I fell in love with. But I didn't like the man he became.

Next, I wanted an auto repair shop. I got it.

But I lost it all after 3 years.

Then I wanted a home on a lake. I got it.

What does this mean? When you want to manifest, be careful what you ask for. Specifics are so important.

Now, there was something I didn't manifest, but for which I was really grateful. I didn't want children. It was a limiting belief that was from my childhood. But I got pregnant even though I had been told that I would never be able to.

Sometimes you don't manifest. But it happens, and it's a gift.

Then after 3 years, and loving my son so much, I wanted more children. Four months later, I was pregnant again, against all odds. And then again, 21 months later.

I believe you CAN manifest your SUCCESS. But YOU HAVE TO TAKE PART in MANIFESTING! It doesn't just happen. YOU HAVE TO BELIEVE.

So BELIEVE. And you NEED TO WANT IT BAD ENOUGH. ☺

So keep going. Send your message out. BELIEVE. MANIFEST through your BELIEF.

BUT to start, YOU HAVE TO BELIEVE IN YOU... and YOU ARE YOUR BRAND!!!

In the interim... create your vision board. And YOUR MAGIC QUESTIONS (book by Bart Baggett, highly recommended: *The Magic Question* ©)

Here are two examples of a "Magic Question" and "Manifesting."

Choose your favorite. But use vision if you are visual. Write on cards if you prefer that method. I have 8: 4 Magic Questions and 4 Manifesting. I figure it doubles my odds. ☺

Magic Question
How amazing is this going to feel?
Top Podcasters
Weekly Podcasts
That Gal With That Guy
"How We See It"
Intested in joining us?
We are on Google Podcast
Tunein, Apple Podcast, Spotify, Stitcher and more!!
I AM THAT GAL

Magic Question
How will I feel when I AM Known for?
Hampy
As a Masters Handwriting Analyst
Handwriting Speaks Volumes
I AM THAT GAL

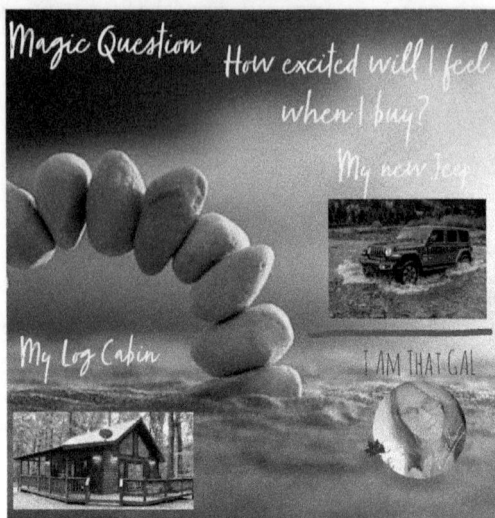

MY FAVORITE NUMBER... 11

CHAPTER 11

WE DEDICATE THIS CHAPTER TO OUR FAMILY IN THE MASTERMIND BRANDING COLLABORATIVE AND ADVANCED BRANDING COLLABORATIVE

This chapter consists of a page from each of our team, who have been there with us for the past year, sharing their opinions of what "collaboration" is.

DEFINITION OF COLLABORATION

by Roy Miller
Member of the Mastermind Branding Collaborative and Founding Member of the Advanced Branding Collaborative

In business, or any other form of enterprise, a collaboration with like-minded individuals is the key to success. I like to think of collaboration as a form of a "mastermind" group. Napoleon Hill was a big proponent of the "Mastermind Principle."

There are so many benefits of collaborating in a group of like-minded individuals. Not only are you able to share your talents and gifts with the other members, you are also able to benefit personally from the other members' talents and gifts. You can edify each other, encourage each other, and share in each other's successes.

When you have collaboration in a group that is working in perfect harmony, toward the same common objective, each person is motivated with enthusiasm, initiative, and strength to persist and accomplish their goals and dreams.

Being a member of The Advanced Branding Collaborative, I have been able to work with some talented people. We all come from different backgrounds, have different skill sets, and are from all over the world. We do share a common heartset of wanting to help people. We want to be able to edify other people and share in their journey to their success, whatever that may be.

Collaborating with the members of this group has inspired me to become a podcaster. One of the group members and I started a podcast together. I am not sure if either one of us would have done this without what we have learned in this group, or by having met each other.

The collaboration in this group has moved all of us into transformation in our business and in our lives, in one way or another. As a matter of fact, one of our members is becoming a transformation coach.

We also have a certified handwriting analyst and grapho-therapist in the group. It is interesting what you can learn from just your signature alone! The insights about your handwriting tell so much about you if you know what to look for. This person is also an author.

Are you interested in NLP (neuro-linguistic programming)? One of our members is a certified NLP coach and hypnotist. She is also a Timeline coach. Do you want to know what in your past is holding you back? She can help you with that.

One of our members is a business coach, public speaker, and author. His expertise comes from over twenty years of experience. Not sure where to start, or what to do? He can help you with that.

Everyone has talents and gifts. You may not see them in yourself, but in a collaborative group, the other members will help you to see them. Learn from each other, share with each other, edify each other, support each other, but most of all, be a contributor.

The exchange of ideas will lead to the exchange of money.

Collaboration
by Wendy Musch
Member of the Mastermind Branding Collaborative and Founding Member of the Advanced Branding Collaborative

What collaboration means to me and why I think it is important:

Let's start with the definition of collaboration.

Collaboration: the process of two or more people or organizations working together to complete a task or achieve a goal.

What does collaboration mean to me?

In the interest of full disclosure, I think that two or more heads are always better than one. One person working alone cannot possibly come up with nearly as many possibilities and ideas as two or more people working together.

To me, collaboration means that people come together to share ideas, resources, solutions, skills, and talents to provide products or services to directly and indirectly help or serve others. I believe this is possible to a far lower degree individually.

Experience has taught me that collaborating with others often provides much more success than working alone. People or teams that work collaboratively, often have access to greater resources, especially in the face of competition with others. Additionally, collaboration generally provides access to a larger audience, and greater recognition, rewards, and success.

Additionally, experience has also taught me that not everyone works well with just anyone and everyone. It is very important to do your due diligence before consenting to or choosing to collaborate with others.

I believe that it is necessary to take your skills, talents, experience, knowledge, and personality into account, as well as those of the other(s) you are considering collaborating with, prior to agreeing to work together. Looking at all these things BEFORE entering a commitment will prevent problems later.

Perhaps it is obvious, but just in case it isn't...make sure that those that you want to collaborate with have services or products that are congruent to yours and the message you are looking to promote. That said, it may not seem like people that have different things to contribute are congruent. However, if you really want to work with someone, there is usually a way to weave different products together to promote the desired message.

It is also helpful, if not necessary, to set parameters at the outset of your collaboration. Doing so will prevent disappointments, issues, and hurt feelings throughout the course of your collaboration.

Collaborations with others may or may not be for you. Remember though, working with others will more often than not provide you with insight, experiences, and ideas that you likely will not come up with on your own. Life is different for everyone, and you will reach more people when you embrace including others in your message, to capture those people that want/need what you have to offer them.

Collaboration
by Jenny Kalz

Member of the Mastermind Branding Collaborative and Founding Member of the Advanced Branding Collaborative

While sitting at my desk on this cold, windy morning, I reflect on what collaboration really means to me.

Over the years, I have learnt that it doesn't matter how many connections you have...

You can know a lot of people but still feel lonely on the inside, and that you are in this by yourself.

What really matters to me is the depth and trust in a relationship.

For a long time, I found it challenging to trust people and to open myself up to be vulnerable within conversations.

The main reason was that I didn't have a strong connection with myself; I had low confidence, was very self-conscious, and was a perfectionist.

Putting myself out there, and risking to be hurt or judged by others, was a big deal for me.

But the more I worked on my own mindset and heartset, the easier it got to open myself up to connect with others: finding people with the same goals; building meaningful connections; lifting each other up, but most importantly, giving each other the permission to be vulnerable; being your true self; stepping into your own greatness; getting to know each other on a deeper level; creating a space where everyone feels safe to share their ideas and receive honest feedback; and having some extra pairs of eyes to see, to wake your dreams into reality.

Another thing I really love about collaboration is that you can connect each other with your network. The other person might know someone that could help you move forward in life or business. And you can do the same thing for them. Networking really is an essential part of business, and through collaboration, you can expand your network of people you know. At the end of the day, it really is about who you know.

What I really love about the Advanced Branding Collaborative is that we have cultivated a very positive environment.

We are all coming from a space of appreciation and gratitude.

And it's so important to have a group of people that lift you up.

When we collaborate with each other, we create a ripple effect and inspire others to become more.

I never thought that I would be able to make great friendships online.

After all, we are all living in different parts of the world and have never met in person. But it is actually the opposite. I have met many great friends and awesome people online. I'm very grateful for technology. It helps us to build our network globally, and to meet people that we would have otherwise never met. So don't hesitate to connect with people online. You never know where that connection may lead to.

I want to personally thank LaurieAnn, Wendy, Robert, and Roy for the last year, for holding me accountable and encouraging me to keep going, and for providing a space for self-expression and growth.

We are all in this together. You don't have to walk this path alone.

Be courageous. Ask for help. Reach out.

Together, we can do so much more. We can build bigger communities, reach more people, have more influence, and help more people to break free and make this world a better place.

MY CHAPTER 12

In Closing

A SPECIAL dedication to the many people in my life that are in my acknowledgments, but I need to share MY definition of collaboration.

A TEXT to a Friend:

Collaboration… sharing, loving, caring, knowing—working together with all of that and more. Being there, answering, questioning; being honest—not brutally but with kind, constructive criticism—being there for each other.

AND? Being a family, a community, and a strong force that works together but not against each other, to make sure the success is realized all around.

Special thanks to Raymond Aaron, Bart Baggett, The Advanced Branding Collaborative Group, and Forbes Riley, for teaching me this in business. And to my mentors, Mom and Dad, Brent Pearce, Wayne Clancy, Doc Grayson, my Pastor Bruxy Cavey, my friends around the world from Montreal, to Istanbul, to London, Ontario, Edmonton, Alberta, Reno, Nevada, Tweed, Ontario and Milton, Ontario (amongst other locations) for teaching this too in my personal world, thank you.

www.ingramcontent.com/pod-product-compliance
Lightning Source LLC
Chambersburg PA
CBHW062009200326
41519CB00017B/4739